The Corporate Color Plan

Henry Leon McNeil

ISBN 979-8-89130-823-7 (paperback)
ISBN 979-8-89130-824-4 (digital)

Christian Faith Publishing
832 Park Avenue
Meadville, PA 16335
www.christianfaithpublishing.com

Printed in the United States of America

Contents

A Struggle for Equality at J&L Steel in PGH, PA

What Really Is the Problem?

Our struggle in J&L Steel/LTV Corporation began by making numerous attempts to get the ear of our corporation's president to establish a meaningful dialogue. The objective was to bring our concerns to that level of management with the large-scale problem of unequal opportunity that existed within J&L the corporation's name in the 1970s.

We realize that the charge of racial discrimination/inequities was commonplace at this time, and we acknowledge that in some cases, such charges are indeed unsupported, if not unfounded. However, we have come to the inevitable conclusion that in our particular company, such discriminatory practices were somewhat normal or you might say tolerated. It is for the following major reasons that we have drawn the foregoing conclusions:

1) For a company of thirty-three thousand employees and five billion dollars in sales, it was startling to find out that there were no Blacks nor had there ever been any Blacks in the entire top four levels of management. These top four levels include more than three hundred (300) individuals, whose ethnic origins traverse almost all nationalities and include White females. The only ethnic background that has been

prohibited from joining this esteemed group of people were those of African heritage or decent.

Our research of the movement within these three top tiers of management (excluding the president) from August 1980 to August 1981 in the Pittsburgh area reveals the following results:

a. Within the one-year period stated above, there were ten (10) promotions into the second level removed from the chief executive officer (CEO), thirty-two (32) individuals were promoted into the third level removed from the CEO. There was a total of forty-two promotions in a one-year period, and not one Black was ever seriously considered for any of these high-level positions. *Is it any wonder why racial oppression has lasted so long?*

b. As for promotions, one could argue from the corporate perspective that "we bring our people up through the ranks." Granted, Blacks have not been properly groomed; however, we maintain that a system of exclusionary policy exists where Blacks are concerned. This system is so well entrenched that few Blacks have had the rare opportunity to share any measure of career success at J&L. The few who have managed to break through at lower levels have eventually encountered the corporation's conservative policies, which caused potential Black executives to resign or have their careers stymie.

2) Our study also revealed that within the same one-year period, ten individuals were hired from outside the company into the second and third levels removed from the CEO. None of these new hires was Black. J&L probably stands alone (in modern times) in its contention that *"we cannot fine a good..."* (*Just to let you know that during the*

1960s and well into the 1980s, this was the personnel department's favorite refrain.)

The facts mentioned above are of particular significance since our company was a major part of the parent company, LTV, and LTV relied heavily on the American taxpayer's dollars to finance its companies. A detail of the amount of defense money spent during the early 1980s via contracts with LTV is as follows:

Total Sales (Millions)	LTV Subsidiaries	Amt of Defense Contract Sales 1981	% of Total Sales
	Vought Corp. &		
$797	Kentron-Aerospace/Defense	$590 million	74%
$6,714	J&L Steel Corp. Continental-Emsco Lykes Steamship	50 million	1%
$7,511		$640 million	

Below is a chart that represents a brief summary of some data we collected that shows just how unequal the job situation at Jones and Laughlin Steel was in 1981.

The *3 Gateway Center* was the headquarters for Jones and Laughlin Steel in 1981. It was situated in downtown Pittsburgh, Pennsylvania.

Aliquippa Works was J&L's largest manufacturing site. It was approximately seven miles long. It was situated along the Ohio River where large barges were used to ship many tons of steel to customers and receive raw material, etc., via barges. This facility was approximately thirty miles north of Pittsburgh.

| At 3 Gateway Center | | | Black | | White | | Other Minorities | Total | | Black % |
Male	Female		Male	Female	Male	Female	Males	White	Black	
221	12	Officials & Managers	2	1	11	219		230	3	1.30%
315	49	Professional, Tech, & Sales	9	5	44	303	3	347	14	4.03%
140	267	Office & Clerical	15	39	228	125	0	353	54	15.30%
676	328	Total Salaried	26	45	283	647	3	930	71	7.63%
	At Aliquippa Works									
885	4	Officials & Managers	29	0	4	856	0	860	29	3.37%
285	32	Professional, Tech, & Sales	9	2	30	275	1	305	11	3.61%
419	134	Office & Clerical	14	17	117	404		521	31	5.95%
1589	170	Total Salaried	52	19	151	1535	1	1686	71	4.21%

Note: Of 233 officials and managers working at headquarters, only three were people of color; that's less than 2 percent. However, the company was handling federal government contracts to the tune of approximately fifteen billion dollars of taxpayers' money.

Note also: As the positions get lower, the minority participation increased but not very much.

When reviewing the above 1981 chart, you can see that our company was operating in a racial discriminatory manner, even when the published signs and various public presentation said otherwise.

The 1981 financial statement projects that Vought Corporation's MLRS (a major subsidiary company of LTV) missile program alone would generate revenues exceeding four billion in a fifteen-year period.[1]

Also, according to LTV's 1981 consolidated financial statement, US government sales increased in 1980 and 1981 by 20 percent and 24 percent respectively. LTV has a Washington, DC office strategically located and well-staffed to ensure that such US government business is continued. We see nothing wrong with any particular company doing business with the government; however, we take issue with any company making so much use of our tax dollars while simultaneously ignoring the black sector in their selection of placement into well-paying jobs. Such blatant bigotry should be forthrightly addressed and investigated.

When we organized in September 1980, we had hoped that the issues mentioned herein could have been addressed internally. Instead, we were met with a series of retaliatory measures by our company delivered ever so carefully, using every legal trick known to mankind to demote, harass, and act otherwise discriminatorily while continuing what J&L believed to be sound, legal reasoning for all their repressive actions.

Below, we have listed only some of our efforts to pursue this situation internally. We have also commented on some actions that have been initiated after we had come to the conclusion that our company did not want to actuate meaningful change. The corporation was stalling for time while the statute of limitations for filing complaints with certain regulatory agencies were expiring on some of the retaliatory acts perpetrated upon the leaders of the J&L Black Caucus and others associated thereto:

____

[1]   Source: US Department of Labor, June 23, 1983, letter from Ellen Shong Bergman, director.

September 30, 1980

A meeting of more than fifty salaried Blacks was held to discuss an internal approach to air our concerns.

From October 1, 1980, through May 1981

We organized and planned our strategy for addressing our concerns. Our concerns were broken down into three broad categories:

A. Top-level management has and is continuing to exclude Blacks from its ranks.
B. The retention rate for Black college graduates is too low due to the discriminate treatment given Blacks.
C. Unequal standards are used in the promotion process.

(*Note*: Some of the following dates listed or elaborated on elsewhere in this book.)

June 15, 1981

J&L Black Caucus representatives sent a letter to the president of J&L, requesting a meeting to address our concerns.

June 25, 1981

A response was written by the general manager of personnel to one of our representatives, which attempted to relegate our concerns to "personal" problems. The general manager suggested the same representative meet with him for a discussion of *his personal* problems.

August 10, 1981

A letter signed by forty salaried Black employees of J&L was again addressed to the company president, expressing our disenchantment about the June 25, 1981, letter and explaining that if we did not get a response from the president by August 15, 1981, it would be clear to us that our request to meet with him had been denied, and all internal efforts would have been exhausted.

August 15, 1981

The J&L Black Caucus scheduled a press conference for Wednesday, August 19, 1981, at the office of the Pittsburgh branch of the NAACP.

August 17, 1981

The company, aware of the impending press conference, summoned each signer of the August 10 letter to their respective personnel offices and asked that each state their *personal problems.*

August 19, 1981

A press conference was held and aired by all three of our major local TV stations and carried by a national wire service.

August 20, 1981

Each signer of the August 10 letter received a form letter from the president, asking us to work with the personnel department.

September 25, 1981

At the request of the personnel department, one of our representatives met with the general manager and delivered what we considered to be problems in the affirmative action area and reasonable proposals for their remedy.

October 16, 1981

The general manager of personnel, responding to our proposals, talked to our representative in broad generalities and was noncommittal about any of our suggestions. He did think it necessary to launch a threat by saying that he did not know how much longer J&L would tolerate the representative's appearances on TV, airing our concerns.

October 23, 1981

Realizing that all internal efforts to resolve these affirmative action problems had failed, our representative sent a letter to the president of the company, expressing concern about several aspects of the October 16 meeting with the general manager.

At this point, we were disappointed and painfully aware that no internal effort would be likely to succeed. Consequently, on November 3, 1981, we filed a class action complaint against the LTV/Jones and Laughlin Steel Corporation with the US Department of Labor's OFCCP/ESA. Almost one year later, in September 1982, OFCCP notified us that they were ready to begin their investigation. This investigation commenced only after direct intervention of a US senator on our behalf.

In June 1982, we sent a letter signed by forty J&L Black employees to the Congressional Black Caucus, in care of Representative Parren J. Mitchell (from the seventh congressional district of Maryland). In this letter, we outlined our problems and requested a fact-finding review, in light of the fact that so much federal funds were being used to help perpetuate a corporation that was practicing overt race discrimination in its employment practices and policies.

We received a reply from Representative Mitchell, dated July 15, 1982, informing us that he had forwarded our correspondence to Representative Walter Fauntroy, chairman of the Congressional Black Caucus. On October 28, 1982, a follow-up letter was sent to Representative Fauntroy, expressing our wish to establish contact with him about our unequal opportunity employment problem. We are not certain if he or other members of the Congressional Black Caucus have had the opportunity to review our problem.

In our attempt to cover all bases, several J&L Black Caucus members filed individual complaints at the Equal Employment Opportunity Commission (EEOC). It was our belief that filing individual complaints was the best way to gain access to Title VII. What we encountered at EEOC was that the complainant was charged with the full burden of proof of discrimination, and therefore, the agency committed itself to little or no investigation of our complaints. In most of the complaint files, the EEOC accepted the company's rationale to interrogatories on prima facie cases of race discrimination and subsequently closed the complaints. In others words, EEOC allowed itself to be totally ineffective and even obstructive in attacking race discrimination at J&L.

We believe that mechanisms exist in this society, which can provide remedy for situations, such as those we were encountering at J&L, but corporate lobbying and politicking has rendered these mechanisms either dormant or ineffective. At this point, even though we realize that we are in an environment that condones employment race discrimination and even rewards it (witness the appointment of Paul Thayer, LTV chairman and CEO, to deputy secretary of defense), we endeavored to press on even more vigorously in our attempts to address the situation.

Introduction

General Preface

Coming from the deep rural south and getting a management training position in a major Fortune 500 company such as J&L Steel Company was a pretty big step for me when you consider the fact that in the city of Pittsburgh, I didn't have a friend or a relative. To be honest, that was one of the reasons I choose Pittsburgh and J&L Steel Company to be my employer. When I was hired, I was told that I had advancement opportunities and was given the usual line by the recruiters that declared they had equal opportunity measures that were publicized and practiced daily. The information about equal opportunity was on almost all of their sales promotion material; it was listed on all the recruiting materials and documents.

Let me be factual about equal opportunity at J&L: There were some members of management who not only took their respective jobs seriously, but believe it or not, I found out that some, not many, of the White folks in the management hierarchy actually wanted to enact policies that reflected equal opportunity for all. Needless to say, these types of folks were ever so rare. They were about scarce as hen's teeth.

However, my approach was to learn what I could from the management training position I was brought in on, and then I was poised to do my best with the skills and knowledge that I possessed after graduating from Alabama State University.

The personnel department was helpful and introduced me to another Black trainee, who was working in the production department in the mill at Aliquippa Works, which was about thirty miles north of Pittsburgh. The guy introduced me to the older lady he was renting a room from in Sewickley, Pennsylvania. And I contracted to rent a room from her. Sewickley was about twenty miles from Pittsburgh, and that meant that I would have a thirty-five-minute ride in to work daily.

The job at J&L Steel was titled financial management trainee. It was deemed to be a very respectable and well-paying job for that day and time.

Basically, I was to spend time in various departments, learning various aspects of accounting for the department that I had been assigned to. And at certain intervals, I was to give an account or report to the vice president of finance, and he would, in turn, tell me how he thought I was doing.

During the first eight months of employment, I was assigned to five or six departments and/or subdepartments, and the learning process varied according to the individual departments.

After eight months working at J&L, I was drafted into the US Army. And after basic training and advance infantry training (AIT), I was ultimately sent and spent a year in Vietnam.

After arriving back home in Camden, Alabama, I observed some very distinct changes that had taken place. When I left in 1969, there was no Negroes in the county courthouse. Even though the US had given Negroes the right to vote through the passing of the civil rights act of 1964, it had no effect on our right to vote until around 1970.

I returned from Vietnam in the summer of 1971 and was pleasantly surprised to see that almost all of the county jobs were now occupied by Negroes. It was now very obvious why the Whites didn't want Blacks to vote because the county was approximately 85 percent Black, and that would mean that in order to get elected, a White person would have to successfully solicit Black votes. Just think about it, you, as a White person, will have to ask the same people you and all the generations before you have treated so offensively to now be your friend and vote for you.

Truly, I am humbled by Black folks' desire to forgive and, in spite of the White man's long-standing history of uncivil and overt atrocities (in the form of lynchings, murders, rapes to name a few) committed against the Black man, we continue to prove our caring nature for all humankind. Let me give you an example that I saw when I returned from Vietnam.

A neighbor, cousin, and close family friend, Mr. James Ephraim, had been elected as one of the first Blacks to hold a county office. As I said before, Wilcox County was approximately 85 percent Black, and that is why the entire board became Black.

Mr. Ephraim heard that I had come back from Vietnam and invited me to sit in on one of their political board meetings to discuss redistricting. Because of their new voting ability, they felt that a segment of our local society (White folks) had been left out of the control of the local government, and being Christians, as most of these elected officials professed to be, they wanted to allow White folks to participate in spite of their low residential voting numbers.

I witnessed the Christian solution they came up with, and it involved requesting the proper state government officials to accept the elected officials' redistricting so the White folks would have a voice in the county government. This effort resulted in creating two seats on the board so the Whites could have a representative voice in Wilcox County government. It is quite interesting and paradoxical that past and present White evangelicals proclaim to espouse such Christian values as "love thy neighbor as thyself" (Mark 12:31). As always, when the opportunity presents itself to use this great command given by our Lord and Savior, Jesus Christ, somehow this group of professed Christians seem to almost always failed to follow God's instructions. I suppose, some think that God prefers one race of folks over another. But again, the scriptures declare that "God is no respecter of persons" (Acts 10:34). This statement simply means that God wants us to understand that He doesn't have favorites among the human race of people. For you see, He created all of us. And since all have sinned and come short of the glory of God, then it stands to reason that we should treat our neighbor (anybody other than ourselves) as we desire to be treated. Ultimately, we are not to judge others, lest we be judged. However, we are to use Scripture in order to handle any and all conflicts.

Remember, you can find out how to deal with those who have sinned against you personally by consulting with Matthew 18:15–17 (KJV):

> Moreover if thy brother shall trespass against thee, go and tell him his fault between thee and him alone: if he shall hear thee, thou hast gained thy brother. But if he will not hear thee, then take with thee one or two more, that in the mouth of two or three witnesses every word may be established. And if he shall neglect to hear them, tell *it* unto the church: but if he neglects to hear the church, let him be unto thee as a heathen man and a publican.

Likewise, when the sin isn't against you personally, but you have observed it, and it is against God's law, then you consult with Galatians 6:1 (KJV):

> Brethren, if a man be overtaken in a fault, ye which are spiritual, restore such an one in the spirit of meekness; considering thyself, lest thou also be tempted.

I've got just a few comments about the so-called religious right (who are almost always of the republican party, which is treated as the republican faith by a great number of them.). These types usually, believe it or not, hide their extreme racial prejudices behind carefully selected passages in Scripture that seem to support their particular twisted view. Now don't get it twisted; I am not saying all evangelical religious right-wing folks are in this twisted category.

A tree is known by the fruit it bears. You have got to wonder what kind of Christian would want to overthrow our democratic-type government, when nobody has ever identified a more perfect government than ours. Suffice it to say, our government allows its citizens so many positive attributes that are lacking in almost every other system of government. Think about it, if you speak out or oppose the top government official in almost all other governments on this earth, you would probably lose your life. Yes, we know there are those who have lost their lives here in the US because of their stance on certain issues, but such persons didn't have their hostile situation sanctioned by the federal government.

I thank God for our laws and statutes that allow our freedom of expression. Were it not for such laws and statutes, I would have been put out of commission long ago.

But just before we get into the nitty-gritty details of the prevailing attitudes of management in the corporate structure, I must have you glance back to the early years. There were hundreds of thousands of press articles and books written, some factual and some fiction, about that period. However, just for a moment, I want to give a brief history on why the progress was so hard, and the achievement vision was so very difficult to see.

Consider a May 17, 1982, *Wall Street Journal* article that highlights "Job-Bias Alert" by Robert Greenberger. This article highlights the fact that federal officials deny that they are backing off from the basic concept of equal employment while acknowledging that much confusion stems from public statements by President Ronald Reagan and administration officials, criticizing the use of federal requirements to redress past job discrimination against minorities and women. In other words, they are saying we acknowledge past race discrimination problems, but we are not willing to make a single sacrifice to address the needed redress. In short or other words, they are saying, in essence, though the problems have had and continue to have lingering negative effects on minorities and women, we don't want to do anything about it; instead we want to maintain the status quo.

You see, it really matters who is president of the United States because affirmative action will travel forward only at the speed designated by the president. It was no secret that President Reagan viewed civil rights and affirmative action in the same light as President Donald Trump. Both of these presidents saw the civil rights struggle as a menace to society and cancerous to their agendas. Sometimes I wonder how someone can sit in a position of extreme power and yet allow a major portion of their constituents to be mistreated systematically by the very government they claim to preside over. "Oh, really!" Well, that's like saying we acknowledge the conundrum that caused you folks to be severely damaged and shortchanged for many generations to come while we, the privileged, were extremely advantaged and, in real time, will continue to benefit socially, politically, financially, and in ways too numerous to mention, yet since any form of reparations would tend to cause some amount of burden for our current White race when they didn't actually inflict this harm on our minority society. Nevertheless, no one can deny that the "bootstraps" that such folk claims they pulled themselves up by was actually created, washed, polished, and shinned by the generations of enslaved Black folks. Ironically, the White House was built with Black slave labor. And so, the White privileged race acknowledges reaping the benefits derived from slave labor and harsh treatment but don't feel the need for reparations.

What's really troubling is that these individuals see themselves as preserving the status quo, while ignoring (or not really caring about) the damage being done to their fellowman in the process. This is the same attitude that facilitated slavery for such a long time. Keep in mind that most slave owners were so-called professed Christians. You must wonder, as I do, just what kind of Christians were these that justify enslaving another human being when knowing about all the human carnage and atrocities, such as rape, severe floggings, beatings, castrations, lynching, and many other detestable acts too numerous to mention in this writing. Yet there is this ever-glowing arrogant and never-ending conceit that always show up whenever the modern-day evangelicals are present. I must admit that I see such ice-cold persons as modern-day pharisees, who want the world to see them as stewards of the moral fiber of America, and I am certain such folks want to be known as people who love our Lord Jesus Christ. But let's see what the Holy Scriptures has to say about the matter:

> If a man say, I love God, and hateth his
> brother, he is a liar: for he that loveth not his

brother whom he hath seen, how can he love
God whom he hath not seen? (1 John 4:20 KJV)

And there you have it, friends and neighbors, God's holy word declaring those who show hatred toward their fellowman couldn't possibly love God. This scripture is not ambiguous; rather, it clearly identifies those who hate their fellowmen as those who don't love God. They are one and the same.

I want not to give the impression that my reflections cast a sour reflection on the entire evangelical world, but if the shoe fits, then wear it.

These are times that really try man's soul. However, there are no simple solutions that will solve systemic hatred of one type or another, but if we, as a humanitarian nation, want to see the playing field level, it can be done.

You know, during discussions about race/ethnicity, some of us tend to think that our particular race or ethnicity encompasses pure bloodlines; well, talk to any real expert on the subject, and you will conclude that there are no such people that have pure bloodlines. This should be easily understood for those who believe the Bible, which indicates that we came from Noah's three descendants: Ham, Shem, and Japheth. Any person who has studied race in an institution of higher learning knows that all of us have some of Ham, Shem, and Japheth in our gene pool. However, I am aware that those who are bent on feeling superior to other categories of people will believe what they have been taught in the society that they grew up in. They believe it because it benefits their physiological and social profile and status. And when you get right down to the numbers, such folks ultimately pulled themselves up by the boots and straps made by our ancestors, the slaves.

When one takes a good look at the human development, and when one has accepted Jesus Christ as their Lord and Savior, then that person will inevitably come to the same conclusion that the framers of our United State Constitution wrote, "All men are created equal," even though some of the framers owned slaves; nevertheless, what they wrote was correct. I believe it is a good idea to believe truth even when the carrier of that truth isn't actually living by it. I thank

God for His truth that is available to all. We really can't use ignorance as an excuse today.

Through various organizations, the Bible has been made available to almost everyone in the world, so it's high time for people to read it with understanding given by the Holy Spirit. I just want you to know that you really should pray to God for a righteous understanding of the sacred scriptures because the Bible (the Word) is God as indicated in John 1:1.

The introduction epilogue: This epilogue will, to some degree, be incomplete in that many significant encounters and relevant events, complaints, corporate injustices, and some significant court rulings were excluded because they were deemed unsuitable for this writing due to a variety of circumstances, including but not limited to the type of outcome that was manifested during the successful legal ruling (in mine and the Caucus favor) by the federal court. Ultimately, my company, LTV Steel, filed for chapter 7 bankruptcy and approximately seventy-seven thousand folks lost their job and not only that, but these unfortunate folks had their retirement pensions *swallowed up/stolen/swindled (pick your choice).* In other words, our pensions (which totaled some few billions of dollars) was deemed more needed by the millionaires on the boards and elsewhere than by those who actually earned and was promised this money. Of course, we know that this nefarious act could have never been accomplished without the aid of our precious US legislators, working hard to satisfy their large corporate lobbyist (code for pay-off artist in these particular type of situations). The truth always brings light to dark untruths.

Before we proceed to the prologue, I must explain that when one begins to understand the corporate system and how it evolves and subsequently develops its direction or, you might say, its nomenclature, you will understand that it was developed by taking a glance at the civil system that it is working in and through. In other words, if the community surrounding the corporate structure has racist views or extremely conservative views and supports a policy of not fairly including minorities in their hiring and promotion agendas, the corporate world will almost always mimic that community because they are a part of said community.

Dealing with Corporate Racism 1970–1990

Prologue: Excerpts of Letters and Meetings from 1978 to 1985 in the Corporate Fight for Equality

February 13, 1978. At the Pittsburgh Press Club, I met with the VP of industrial relations, John Kirkwood, and VP of publicity, John Purser. At this meeting, these gentlemen requested that I submit suggestions to them with respect as to how I perceived J&L equal opportunity as it relates to Blacks. They also suggested that I could possibly submit some résumés of qualified Blacks to them for their consideration. (See reference, page 37 Pre-exile efforts and Page 48 Report to my fellow employee.)

February 21 through-May 26, 1978. Four letters were written to high-level personnel VIPs and managers and had *six meetings* with these same individuals. In both the letters and the meetings, the company representatives defended its policies and procedures as operating in the equal opportunity mode, where Blacks and White females were concerned.

May 17 and 18 of 1978. With the expressed consent of the VP of industrial relations (Mr. Kirkwood), I traveled with personnel representatives to Xavier University and Norfolk State Colleges in an effort to help J&L recruit Black candidates for corporate jobs in J&L.

1

(I was later informed that though some were invited in, none were hired.) (See reference page 40 Pre-exile efforts.)

June 19, 1978, through December 13, 1978. I was abruptly *exiled* to Houston, Texas, where the company had a pipe division. I worked in their accounting department and to the chagrin of some corporate officials. I continued my contact with the corporate personnel department head, just as I had been instructed some months hence by the VP of industrial relation. (See reference page 40 Exile to Texas.)

October 17, 1978. I was ordered to report in Pittsburgh to the director of internal audit (my boss). He questioned me in great details about my affirmative action (as it relates to Blacks) efforts. I reaffirmed that by staying in touch with the VP of industrial relations (via phone calls), I was only following his request to me as we left our last face-to-face meeting. I also wrote a letter to Mr. Delmore detailing the affirmative action as it relates to Blacks. In the letter, I talked in great detail about at least seven recent meetings with various department heads and outlining several areas where Blacks were seemingly being ignored for promotions/advancements. (See ref. page 40 post-exile fight.)

December 13, 1978: Texas exile ended. I was summoned to come back to Pittsburgh. But after the Christmas holidays and the beginning of the new year, I received a word from my director on *February 1, 1979,* to report to the acting VP if finances and was shocked to be informed by him that some positive actions was about to be taken after finding and acknowledging that some corporate affirmative shortcomings sited in one of my letters were actually true. To my surprise, there was a substantial increase in the Black clerical workforce at the Plaza where I worked and also about three (3) exempt (management types) Blacks who were hired. (See ref. page 40 post-exile fight.)

September 19, 1979. The audit manager held a three-hour meeting with the senior auditors. He started by talking in general, then he talked about what he really called the meeting for, and that was to announce that he was reorganizing and had plans to make some senior auditors supervising senior auditors. He had already expressed his dissatisfaction with my affirmative action concerns, and as I suspected, I was not selected to be one of the supervising senior auditors. I am not suggesting that he made his decision in a biased fashion; I'm just saying.

Threat of retaliation for my concerns, February 8, 1980. My boss, the audit manager, angrily said he would no longer prove anything to me about affirmative action and further said he would discuss it at my evaluation.

More hopeful signs by J&L, February 12, 1980. I sent a follow-up letter to VP Kirkwood on affirmative action as it relates to Blacks. The letter acknowledges three positive changes since my October 14, 1978, midexile report to the audit manager.

Adding insult to injury, February 15, 1980. My audit manager informed me that he thought I didn't write the February 12, 1980, letter to Mr. Kirkwood because, as he put it, it was too smooth. He said he thought I was being used. *Is it any wonder why race discrimination is so hard to get rid of?*

February 25, 1980. I responded to the above situation with a letter to my audit manager, expressing my disappointment with his attempt to discredit my letter about affirmative action. A copy of the handwritten five-page letter I wrote to Mr. W. C. Anderson is offered below:

Dear Bill,

When you received my letter addressed to Mr. Kirkwood the other day, you came into my office and expressed your belief that I did not write the letter. You said it was too "smooth" for me to have written.

At first, I was elated to learn that you thought my letter was well written. Shortly thereafter, I realized that you had insulted my intelligence, and I had accepted it as a compliment (knowing I had constructed it [the letter]).

So why is my manager saying I do not have enough intellect to construct such a document?

You went on to suggest that I was being used as a tool for others or someone else.

Perhaps there are those who might gain from what I am trying to do. However, after all the letters, meetings, headaches, and the likes, it is inconceivable that you would think that I would put myself through such torture at the behest of others. Such behavior befits imbeciles.

It is commonly thought that Blacks too often interpret personal or "constructive" criticism as being a form of racism. It is moot to argue this assertion. Nevertheless, racism lives on in most of our hearts.

The accusation that my letter was not authentic, and the assertion that I am being used are discreditable statements that I had expected from J&L's Personnel Department. I must admit, it grieved me much to have heard such things coming from you.

When I decided to embark on this Affirmative Action concern two years ago, I knew that I would be met with strong opposition. It is pleasant to think of that time in the future, when one can go to work daily and not have to be concerned with skin color.

As it stands now, we are all concerned with race one way or another.

Sincerely,
Henry L. McNeil

March 6, 1980. I expressed my dissatisfaction to my audit manager during the evaluation and being passed up for a supervising senior position.

Promotion, March 21, 1980. I was promoted to the position of area supervisor-general and maintenance at Pittsburgh Works Accounting.

Update to the Caucus, June 16, 1980. I wrote a letter to the J&L Black Caucus to inform them of all of our recent activities concerning our quest for the company to actually live up to its written creed to actuate equal opportunity for all of its employees and not just sloganize equal opportunity to suit and just patronize those interested in true reform in the way companies hire and treat Blacks. (See reference page 48 Report to my fellow employees.)

The Caucus ramping up its activities, December 19, 1980. in a meeting attended by sixty caucus members, we decided to increase our efforts to achieve equal opportunity at the workplace.

January 15, 1981. from our group, Thomas Bigelow, Lorraine Williams, and Henry McNeil wrote a letter to the president of J&L, requesting a meeting with him.

January 30, 1981. I was summoned to a meeting with the general manager of personnel and J&L's top-ranking lawyer. They attempted to have me respond to a letter that they said that I wrote. Since they wouldn't tell me from whence they got the letter, I simply responded by letting them know that I certainly didn't send a letter to either of them and was certain I was not going to discuss a letter I wrote to someone else. So that was that. February 2, 1981, I sent a narrative of this January 30, 1981, meeting to the following, copying the president of J&L, VP of industrial relations of J&L, assistant controller of J&L, senior vice president personnel of LTV (parent company), manager personnel of J&L, and VP and general counsel of LTV.

Taking it to the streets, March 14, 1981. I held a Caucus meeting at Homewood Branch Library, where Mr. Bob Pitts of the local NAACP spoke to us. (See reference page 37 Force to take it public via press conference.)

Demoted but still determined, March 27, 1981. I was called in to meet with Eastern division comptroller and the Pittsburgh works comptroller (Mr. Eichenlaub and Mr. Perlik), where I was informed that I was being demoted to the supervisor of the Hazelwood

Information Control Center. As always, they put it under the label of restructured workplace, which was a common term used when a person was to be demoted. Nevertheless, I left the meeting more determined than ever to pursue equal opportunity for Blacks in our company.

April 3, 1981. I met with R. E. Grieve, VP of finance of LTV, and filed a verbal complaint about the impending demotion that I viewed as corporate retaliation for my affirmative action concerns. He said he would look into it. I followed up this meeting with an April 22, 1981, letter to Mr. Grieve.

May 1, 1981. I received a letter from J. E. Eichenlaub, responding to my April 3, 1981, meeting with the VP of finance of LTV by stating that Mr. Grieve was satisfied that the restructuring, including my demotion, was proper.

June 4, 1981. I received an unfair and a less than objective evaluation from Mr. J. E. Eichenlaub, serving as the Pittsburgh Work Controller, to which I gave an oral rebuttal.

Divide and conquer tactic move by corporate, June 25, 1981. Mr. D. L. Carroll wrote a letter to Mr. T. Bigelow, one of three signers of a recent letter to President Thomas C. Graham, requesting a meeting with our group to discuss our assertions of unequal employment at J&L, where Blacks were concerned. In Mr. Carroll's letter, he suggested that our concerns were of a personal nature and wanted to arrange a meeting solely and only with Mr. Bigelow. Of course, this was clearly and unsuccessful attempt to divide and conquer the Caucus.

The Caucus response on August 10, 1981. Forty Caucus members signed a letter addressed to the J&L president, whereupon we informed him that his representative had misrepresented our concerns by claiming such concerns were of a personal nature. We respectfully asked the president to respond to our letter by August 15, 1981.

The decision to go public on August 15, 1981. When we didn't hear from the company president by August 15, as we had requested, and after thirty-four incidents of letters and meetings during the previous one and a half years, the J&L Black Caucus voted to hold a press conference to take the J&L unequal employment issue public. (See reference page 37 Force to take it public via Press Conf.)

The company called each letter signer on August 17, 1981. The company's personnel division called each signer in under the pretense that they wanted to hear what the concerns were. This act only confirmed the fact that our efforts to have our company achieve a greater and more sincere level of affirmative action were being systematically maligned by the "powers that be."

The press conference, August 19, 1981. The J&L Black Caucus held a press conference at the NAACP Hill District Pittsburgh Office, where we took our unequal employment issues public. All three of the local TV news personnel came to hear, record, and publish our concerns. (See reference page 51, press release, August 19, 1981.)

The president's letter, August 20, 1981. The president sent a letter to each of the forty signers of the August 10 letter. His letter had a lot of words that said and committed to absolutely nothing we had requested. He didn't even agree to meet with any or all of us.

September 25, 1981. I was interviewed on TV by a TV personality on the show called *Vibrations.* The interview was an open discussion about the racist policies and practices that I alleged were in use at J&L Steel. Various personnel representatives voiced their distaste for the show, and that was understandable.

Addressing threats from company, October 23, 1981. I sent a letter to President Graham and personnel, stating that I would continue to expose the truth about our company. I said I was prepared to sacrifice my job and even my life if that was the price I must pay to exercise my First Amendment rights guaranteed to US citizens by our constitution.

Note, the December 31, 1981, letter below that I sent to R. A. Perlik, Eastern division controller of J&L. The letter was needed in order to establish the fact that my looking into affirmative action, as it relates to Black, was done with the knowledge and consent of the personnel department. This letter would clear up a few things that lingered in my mind since I was summoned to a November 11, 1981, meeting that included J. E. Eichenlaub and J. Drotos.

At this ten-minute meeting, I was informed that the personnel department had decided to discontinue our Affirmative Action dialogue. I was not accused of any misconduct.

It was at Mr. Carroll's request that arrangements were made, whereby he and I could discuss affirmative action as it related to Blacks in J&L. The same request was made by the personnel department in 1978 under the direction of another general manager. But after a brief period, that gentleman decided he no longer wanted such a dialogue with me. He informed my supervisor (J. Delmore) that said, dialogue must now be discontinued.

As of my October 23, 1981, the letter to Messrs. T. C. Graham (president of J&L) and D. L. Carroll, I constructed it using my own time. I could not spare the time to construct it while supervising the Hazelwood ICC. I felt the use of J&L letterhead was appropriate because the letter was part of the dialogue established by Mr. Carroll.

Finally, as far as I was concerned, this matter was closed. I would continue to honor their requests concerning these matters. The above was constructed at home, on my own time. No J&L material was used.

—H. L. McNeil

Cc: Gen. Mgr., Personnel; Mgr., Personnel-Pgh. Wks.; Controller, Pgh. Wks.; V. P. Ind. Relations; and Mgr. Personnel

Caucus decided to seek redress in court, November 3, 1981. After observing much company disingenuous rhetoric, our Caucus voted to seek redress to our civil rights/unequal employment situation in the various civil courts systems. Approximately twelve complaints were filed with the EEOC.

November 9, 1981, I received yet another threatening letter from Mr. Carroll, suggesting that my concern for Black employees at J&L was outside of the scope of my job responsibilities. What was so messed up about his comment is the fact that affirmative action must have been outside the scope of his job responsibilities too, judging by his deliberate inaction seen in his steadfast dedication to the old status quo. The status quo was to post affirmative action slogans on all publications, signs, and even billboards and do absolutely nothing to correct the prevailing systemic injustice.

November 12, 1981. The corporate trio: the works controller, division controller, and the personnel manager met with me about my job responsibilities and at the same time tried to play down the threatened nature of Mr. Carroll's recent letter to me.

November 27, 1981. The Caucus was notified that our claims filed against J&L would be investigated by the Pittsburgh Office of Federal Contract Compliance Programs.

April 15, 1982. At my request, a recently hired Black exempt personnel met with me to discuss something that she had said to one of my closest advisers, Gwen Howze. (The Caucus believed this recently hired exempt personnel was hired solely to keep tabs on the J&L Black Caucus. She really didn't try hard to hide that fact.) Anyway, what she had said to Gwen the previous day was disturbing to me, and I had to let her know that I thought she was out of line. Part of the reason I arranged this meeting with her was to inform her that I was well aware of the fact that keeping us (the J&L Black Caucus) in line was solely the reason she was hired. I could not claim victory from this meeting; however, I left the meeting feeling somewhat better.

Visited Weirton Black Caucus as their guest, September 26, 1982. Five of our key members visited this group for about five hours. It was sobering to learn that our experiences with unequal employment was not unique but rather systemic for the country.

Seeking another avenue of redress, October 3, 1982. Seeing that progress was not forthcoming from the EEOC, we approached the Office of Federal Contract Compliance Program (OFCCP) and asked for help with our cases.

November 28, 1982. I sent a letter addressed to Ms. Jane S. Harris, equal opportunity specialist US Department of Labor OFCCP Pittsburgh area office, enclosing at least thirteen letters written to or received from EEOC Pittsburgh and Philadelphia District Offices concerning redress for members of the J&L Black Caucus.

January 13, 1983. At 4:00 p.m., I met with OFCCP representative who said the OFCCP probably would not investigate because of two cases already opened with the EEOC.

January 21, 1983. At 11:05 a.m., an OFCCP representative claimed that if a class action suit had not been filed, the OFCCP would keep investigating.

January 31, 1983. At 4:25 p.m., I received a phone call from OFCCP representative, saying that they would only proceed with two cases (Gwen and Elmer).

February 17, 1983. At 4:18 p.m., I met with Lawyer J. Hardiman about the cases.

February 24, 1983. I wrote a letter to the US Department of Labor under the Freedom of Information Act, requesting copies of the Equal Employment Opportunity, Employer Information Reports (EEO-1) that was routinely submitted by the company.

Faced civil roadblocks, February 22, 1983. I received a letter from OFCCP, indicating two members were issued Right to Sue (meaning that the agency found reasonable grounds to believe racial discrimination had taken place.) We subsequently file these two cases with the US District Court of Western Pennsylvania. Two other cases remained opened. One was found to be untimely, and one was withdrawn by the complainant.

February 24, 1983. I sent a letter to the US Department of Labor, requesting copies of the Equal Employment Opportunity, Employer Information Reports (EEO-1) that had been routinely submitted by J&L Pittsburgh and Aliquippa Works.

March 2, 1983. I received a letter from the OFCCP, officially concluding their noninvestigation by citing bureaucratic gobbledygook, repeating the same results stated in their February 22 letter.

March 4, 1983. I wrote a three-page rebuttal to the EEOC investigator, who was handling my particular case. I responded to at least four inaccurate assertions made by J&L to EEOC during their extremely limited investigation.

Contacted our US senator (Mr. Arlen Specter), March 15, 1983. In this letter, we (the J&L Black Caucus) complained about the

OFCCP and other federal agencies that claimed to promote equal opportunity while actually promoting status quo.

May 4, 1983. A second letter was sent to Senator Specter, asking him to intercede on our behalf with the secretary of the US Department of Labor to grant OFCCP the freedom to investigate our charges via an in-depth compliance review, despite the artificial barrier presented by Consent Decree II. Our complaint alleged that Consent Decree II was an artificial barrier created by politicians in conjunction with so-called lobbyist to shut down those who complain about such things as race and other types of discrimination. To put it bluntly, such decrees were designed to be a safe way to acquire influence without actually calling it that as such.

June 6, 1983. I received a June 2, 1983, letter from the Director of Employment Standards Administration of the OFCCP in answer to our February 24, 1983, letter requesting EEO-1 reports. Ms. Bergman said that they had 1979 and 1981 EEO-1 reports for both Pittsburgh and Aliquippa facilities, but we couldn't get the reports until the contractor (J&L) be given the opportunity to object to the release of these documents. Well, here we go again with sophisticated bureaucratic roadblocks that hinder nonrich folks from achieving any essence of equality in the workplace. The statistical data we received showed unbelievable low percentages of Black employees in all of the well-paying jobs and jobs of significant responsibility.

June 23, 1983. I received another letter from Mr. Bergman in response to our February 24, 1983, letter, saying that although they had indicated they had the 1979 EEO-a report for J&L; however, they were not able to locate it. So we had to summarize data sources on our own. (And we wonder why our government is accused of being wasteful. Oh! but wait, they are being very helpful to those entities that continue to operate in a racial discriminatory manner.)

June 27, 1983. We received a letter from Senator Arlen Specter, saying that an inquiry to the Office of Federal Contract Compliance Programs had been initiated on our behalf. He ended that letter by saying that he would contact us as soon as he received a response from the agency.

July 15, 1983. We received a copy of a July 15, 1983, letter from OFCCP, written to Senator Specter. The Pittsburgh Office of the OFCCP did exactly what they were put in place to do, and that is to *stop* or *shut down* any attempts to investigate or, as they put it, conduct a compliance review of J&L. They refused to investigate this corporation, which had fifteen billion dollars in government contracts funded by taxpayers' dollars. They supported their dereliction of duty by citing (1) some vague system that they referred to as the Equal Employment Data System (EEDS) with no explanation of how corporations were selected for review. (2) In addition, they cited the fact that J&L was part of the Steel Consent Decree, which they claim, limited their ability to conduct reviews of companies covered. Well, here we go again with sophisticated bureaucratic roadblocks that hinder nonrich folks from achieving any essence of equality in the workplace.

August 19, 1983. We received a letter from Senator Specter, attaching a reply from the Department of Labor in response to his inquiry on our behalf. The reply that Senator Specter referenced was the noncommittal letter from OFCCP cited above.

January 30, 1984. After many meeting with our lawyers, the Caucus decided to appeal two of our twelve cases to a higher court (Alex Jones and Gwen Howze).

January 30, 1984, through April 21, 1984. The Caucus met with our lawyers to plan court strategies of the active cases.

Off to federal court, May 21, 1984. One of our Caucus members, Anna Jones, brought a race discrimination civil suit under title 7 to the United States District Court for the Western District of Pennsylvania. There was testimony by several fellow employees, as well as company officials.

To God be the glory. David vs. Goliath—David wins.

July 25, 1984. The District Court for the Western District of Pennsylvania ruled in favor of the Plaintiff, Anna Jones.

Justice will not be denied when Jesus Christ is injected into the situation. (Much prayer was submitted to Almighty God.) *To God be the glory.*

To God be the glory. David vs. Goliath—again, David wins.

December 28, 1984. The United States Court of Appeals for the Third Circuit *set aside* and *overturned* the district court, granting summary judgment in favor of the defendant, Jones & Laughlin Steel Corporation. This ruling was the results of Alex Jones and Gwen Howze cases being argued by our lawyer, Attorney Thomas J. Henderson, on *September 10, 1984.* Both of these Caucus members went on to win their cases in the Third Circuit Court of Appeals. *God is able and will see you through!*

March 10, 1985. The Caucus discussed how we should view what we perceived as unfair or biased annual evaluations. We recognized annual evaluations as one of the weapons the company had at its disposal to use as a tool to retaliate against those who challenged their equal opportunity policies and practices.

April 6, 1985. EEOC found cause to believe the Black Aliquippa guards were victims of race discrimination.

May 27, 1985. I wrote a nineteen-page rebuttal to my supervisor's annual evaluation of me.

Affirmative Action during Plant Closings

July 8, 1985. I wrote letters to (1) R. A. Perlik, controller of the remnant of Pittsburgh Works J&L/LTV and (2) A. Cole Tremain, VP of industrial relations J&L/LTV Essentially, I informed these gentlemen that I had notice a recent and disturbing trend of excluding Blacks from consideration for continued employment in our company in areas where shutdowns and idle plant activity was taken place. I cited the fact that I was the only person remaining at Pittsburgh Work accounting with a four-year college degree while all of the Whites with such degrees had been transferred to other locations. I cited several other apparent discriminatory practices that were taken place.

July 31, 1985. received a replay from Mr. A. Cole Tremain to my July 8, 1985, letter using all the official corporate responses that usually satisfied those who really weren't looking for real answers or solutions to the problem of unequal employment opportunity. Nevertheless, he did reply.

October 25, 1985. Gwen Howze accepted a new position at another location as part of the settlement of the civil rights lawsuit that she won.

Slow Incremental Change

Please note that the following six points are written so those who are not familiar with the preseventies' general Southern Jim Crow south can try to understand what the prevailing attitudes of those officials, who were in complete control of our well-being or troubled lives as the case may be. When talking with some folks who were brought up in the northern part of our America, we find that they have difficulty understanding what the fuss is all about. Their misunderstanding is not necessarily due to racial bias but is more likely attributed to ignorance. Below, I have outlined six basis points that should shed some light on this situation. I realize that though we are patriotic brothers and sisters, some of our experiences as US citizens have been extremely different from what the norms should be. These experiences often have served to determine who goes up and who goes down. These varied experiences have often been labeled as discriminatory, and as such, there are those who would dare to suggest that these rude and ungodly practices had nothing to do with their wealth and general welfare. I cringe when I hear some folks saying that they pulled themselves up by their bootstraps. In any case, the following points should explain a few things about why one, such as I, would dare offer a challenge to a fifteen-billion-dollar corporation without visible legal representation.

Why Southern Blacks were attracted to the northern part of the US

Some facts might be glossed over in our current day, but I intend to expose them because they are important in understanding why racial discrimination was and still is so difficult to understand and reckoned with.

It is worth noting and establishing some basic or fundamental reasons I and others like me, who had received a college education from a Southern institution of higher learning during the 1960s and 1970s, migrated to the Northern US in the first place. First, it must be noted that during that period of time, every moment of a Southern child's life was in peril primarily because of many factors. Below, I will list a few of the more prevalent and disturbing circumstances:

1. *Because the state and local laws deliberately and blatantly favored the White society.*

In those days, these lily-white legislatures didn't even bother nor have enough respect for Black folks to try and cover up discrimination as they do now. Let me give just one example: When I was in grade school (they called it elementary school back them), I was in the local town (Camden, Alabama) when a White man accidentally ran into my father's parked car. When my father came to the car, the White man looked him with a sober-like face and said: "Sol [that was my father's name], I will let you know how much you owe me." The White man said this because he knew the law gave him 100 percent protection and gave no such liberties to any person of color. This isn't something I read in a book. No! No! I am writing from personal experience.

In those days, the state and local laws were deliberately codified not in a subtle way but rather in a deliberate way so that there would be no doubt that whenever there was Black against White, White was automatically the winner in whatever situation that might have been in question. Clearly, in those days and at that place (Camden, Alabama), the laws were made to favor the White man.

2. *Such laws couldn't be changed because people of color were not permitted by law to vote.*

One of the ways they skirted around the constitution was by declaring people of color not to be humans. Many Whites, if not most, actually believed that lie. I guess it is easy to believe a lie that benefits you. You see, the forgoing actually highlights that important biblical command:

> Train up a child in the way he should go:
> and when he is old, he will not depart from it.
> (Proverbs 22:6 KJV)

3. *Racial prejudice was taught at an early age to both Black and White children.*

When children are brought up and raised in the toxic environment of racial bigotry and biasness, they will naturally believe that the White race of people are superior to any other race because that is what they have been taught all through their formative years of life (ages one to six and beyond) and they witness the grossly unequal treatment, the untold amount of rape, physical, and mental abuse that was such a common factor of our daily life. Did you not know that murdering a Negro was actually thought of as a cleansing of the human race, and many of the so-called Christians actually found Scripture that, in their twisted mind, supported these terroristic acts? What was really sick about this situation was that not only did the Whites teach their children but that they were born to a superior race. I am particularly ashamed of the fact that many of our Black parents taught their children to develop inferiority complexes. This teaching was done in many ways—for instance, always answering the White person with "yessur" or "norsir" with their heads bowed down. If a Black male looked into the eyes of a White female, it could result in castration or, even worse, death by lynching. Our upbringing was as close to slavery as you could possibly get. It really was neoslavery.

I am not proud of the fact that I wasn't really embracing my blackness until somewhere in the 1960s, James Brown made the song called "I'm Black and I'm Proud." It's truly amazing how you can be subconsciously brainwashed into disliking the very hue God has ordained for your physical stature.

At this point, I want to inform you that even though I grew up in the Jim Crow southern rural area, just six months after my brother Sol and I graduated from high school in 1964, the local (Camden, Alabama) civil right struggle officially began, and many brave Black souls got involved and as a result, some were killed, many were arrested, and a number of folks were put off their rented land (usually sharecroppers) and there were a number of Blacks who was too afraid to challenge the system. I want to point out just one documented case of official systematic racial retaliation for those who would dare to challenge. This case involved Reverend Frank Smith, BS, MEd, and DD, whose teaching contract was terminated in 1965 by the Wilcox County (Alabama) school board because he was involved in the local civil rights struggle. The Alabama State Tenure board ruled the dismissal illegal. When the case was brought to the local court (there were no Blacks in the local court system in those days) in the spring of 1968, the clerk of court mysteriously lost all the records. Later, when the case was brought up in court, no one gave notice to Reverend Smith nor his lawyer, and the judge ordered the case closed.[2]

The case cited above represented only one of the many injustices inflicted on those who had the unmitigated gall to challenge the status quo "Jim Crow System."

As I have indicated elsewhere in this writing, I am truly amazed at those folks who hold claim to be of the Christian faith while embracing terror as long as such applies to people that they have been taught to dislike or those that have been dehumanized in their mind, and subsequently, they feel no compassion for such people and actually somehow think such is befitting the Christian walk. It was

---

[2] Gwendolyn Smith, *Why Stand Up?* (Nashville, TN: Choice Publishing,), page 86.

this kind of twisted thinking that caused the attempted January 6, 2021, insurrection on our United States capitol.

It is so easy to hate others when that hating seems to benefit you in some tangible way. The hatred displayed at the capitol during the insurrection attempt was prompted and pushed on by the president of the United States, Mr. Donald Trump. This man is simply power drunk; he really doesn't care so much about his party agenda or any other political platform. He simply wants to be king.

He couldn't care less about what the democrats or the republicans want as a platform as long as he is chosen king. If such misfortune would become a reality, he will be happy as a pig in slop. But let's move on to some of the more pertinent reasons for our slow progress in making a turn for equal opportunity in the corporate sectors of our society.

4. *People are turning away from God. They have abandoned the God that brought them through slavery.*

Just as the Old Testament Children of Israel did many times after God had intervened on their behalf and brought them through insurmountable obstacles, Blacks have, in large numbers, abandoned God's laws and covenants and are now turning to a more worldly approach to solving our problems. It's sad to see so many of our so-called leaders turn their back on God and somehow think that Christianity and a devout belief in Jesus Christ is no longer relevant.

But we must remember what Jesus said to the church at Ephesus:

> Nevertheless I have somewhat against thee, because thou hast left thy first love. Remember therefore from whence thou art fallen, and repent, and do the first works; or else I will come unto thee quickly, and will remove thy candlestick out of his place, except thou repent. (Revelation 2:4–5 KJV)

In this passage, God is telling them that they must remember to cherish the first love. The love they had for one another and, most importantly, the love they had for Christ Jesus.

The message is clear, it was God who brought you through the rough times, and less you repent, you will fall again onto extremely hard times and will not be successful in your endeavors.

There shall never be an age so modern and so new that it should abandoned God. For God is the Creator and Maker of all. How dare you seek to do away with our Christian tenants of faith? How does one exist without being created?

5.   *Change is often uncomfortable*

Change is often uncomfortable because we are being asked to move away from comfortable ways and habits. In the case of race changes, it becomes very difficult for several reasons. It is difficult because of our upbringing, naturally perceived different social status, our perceived physical differences, our social/economic status, how society in general sees us.

The Old South was not willing to make changes that would cause them to lose all of the racial privileges they and their many previous generations had so vigorously held on to, even at the cost of many lives. The truth is that much of this Old South thinking still prevails today. You can see a lot of it in and around Mr. Donald Trump and his followers. This leads us right into the subsequent topic.

6.   *Things not to do when challenging*

a)   *Don't underestimate the opponent's*
       -knowledge—because if he knows more about you than
                you are aware of, you will head in the direction of
                failure and not be aware of it.
       -positional strength—this is strength by virtue of the
                position they hold and how that position relates
                to you.

b) *Don't let your challenge be sideswiped* by the accusation that you are playing the race card. You see the race card was designed by Whites for their specific use. It's been said many times that a good *defense* is often routed in actuating a vigorous *offense*, which is designed to take the focus away from their vile and corrupt discriminatory activity and shines the light of motive suspicion directly on you.

Also, please be careful who you have in your inner circle, for it is from the inside that the smartest opponent seeks to infiltrate. This tactic was used by Jesus Christ's opponents. (Although, I must inform you that what they were trying to do had been revealed in scripture many centuries before.) They gained access to one of His disciples, Judas, to try to take our Lord and Savior, Jesus Christ, down. All the enemy was doing by this act was fulfilling scripture that had been prophesize hundreds of years before by such prophets as Isaiah, Micah, and others. In our Caucus, we experience an attempt by the top brass to isolate and thereby intimidate our inner circle. The individual was asked to be the initial point person when we made our first written approach to J&L's upper echelon leadership. What followed was an attempt by the company to try to make this gentleman's approach personal and thereby negate all the Black Caucus's efforts to launch a successful challenge to the company's systematic raciest policies.

The Caucus quickly recognized the company's failed attempt and wrote a follow-up letter signed by forty-two Caucus members and thereby letting the company know that we "might have been born at night but not last night." The individual we sent to represent us was later fired, or he left the company of his own will. (We really don't know which, and for some reason, our attempts to find out failed.) We moved on. Anyway, we quickly recognized their attempt to sideswipe and marginalize our efforts, and we moved forward and kept pushing our way forward in spite of this company effort to nullify our concerns.

How to effect change

First of all, this part of the message is succinctly addressed to the oppressed, the underserved, underutilized. In other words, we are talking to those whose best interest would be served by the changes you are trying to affect.

Know this: If you are a member of the highly privileged group, it isn't readily apparent what the advantages are for you to fight against those privileges. Let's face it; it is certainly human nature, as we think of it, to want an advantage in just about every situation. Even Jesus's closest disciples wanted certain privileges or advantages over His other disciples. See what two of His disciples did in Mark 10:35–37 (KJV) was asking:

> And James and John, the sons of Zebedee,
> come unto him, saying, Master, we would that
> thou shouldest do for us whatsoever we shall
> desire. And he said unto them, *what would ye that
> I should do for you?* They said unto him, Grant
> unto us that we may sit, one on thy right hand,
> and the other on thy left hand, in thy glory.

And there you have it, the human nature in James and John made them feel like they should have special privileges because they felt that they were in a situation where such could be granted to them, and it was their intentions to have the requested privilege.

Change cannot happen without the following:

Reality 1

1. Educating the oppressor on the need and subsequent advantages of a shift in the normal paradigm and showing this group the long-term effects of this course that you have charted. In *Reality 1*, the oppressor needs to be convinced (hopefully in a peaceful way) to *move away the convenience status quo paradigms.*

2. Educating the oppressed on their need to be consistently moving away from the status quo and enlisting God's help for equal opportunity. The oppressed must understand the enormous power we possess simply by being on the right side of the situation and, most importantly, knowing that God is on our side.

Reality 2

In *reality 2*, the oppressed can't ever give up because he is being abuse, confused, and underused by the current status quo paradigm. You see, for him, a change is imminent.

3. Finally, the oppressor and the oppressed are called upon to work together with great sensitivity and respect even for the legitimacy of the cause that is being pursued. All could benefit from a lesson on respecting others' views that don't necessarily agree with their own.

Reality 3

In *reality 3*, both groups are call upon to work together respectfully, to search, find, and implement changes that will result in fairness and consequently bring long-term positive results for the general society represented by both groups.

As I bring all three *realities* together, we will most assuredly see resounding progress. To summarize: When the oppressor is convinced that his best mode of survival is to move away from the status quo, knowing that the oppressed has found it unbearable and consequently for the good of all parties thereto, he will move away from the status quo to a more reconciliatory position of working together for the greater good.

One needs to recognize the difficulties of giving up some centuries of racial advantages that allowed people of one particular group to rape, at will, members of another ethnicity and even kill any interested party connected (such as the husband). The acts of violence and uncivil behavior by the oppressor were even justified via some of the religious leaders. Even in my lifetime, these acts were still being carried out.

And so, with all of this history of systemic wrongdoing, the oppressor becomes comfortable in his position of handing out racial inequality on a full and wide scale basic.

When you consider the situation, it is no wonder it has taken some four hundred years to effect change, and even now we have some people in high political positions trying very hard to "hold their knees on our necks."

If you were to examine the in-depth lives of those persons storming the capital in an attempted insurrection on January 6, 2021, you will find that most of these Trump supporters were so eager to slow down the process of granting equal opportunities that they simply couldn't bear the thought of being on equal footing with any so-called minority. After all, seventy-four million folks voted for Mr. Donald Trump to be president, and I support their right to vote for whoever they want to; however, a large portion of these same people have and are still doing everything in their power to deny minorities or people of color equal rights that are long overdue.

I heard one great speaker (I believe it was Reverend Dr. Martin Luther King) say that through the constitution, the United States wrote a check to the citizens of our great nation, promising liberty and justice for all. It is a crying shame that Blacks are still waiting to be able to cash that check and enjoy the freedoms it promises, such freedoms that others have always enjoyed. It's time to get on with the business of equal opportunity for all!

Reflection on the realities: During the seventies and eighties, those in control of TV ads had accepted a very limited number of Blacks in their commercial ads; however, the construct of their ads was extremely restricted, i.e., (a) you would never see an ad where the so-called races were mixed unless they were of the same gender (and that too, was rare), (b) Rarely were there ever any ethnic groups other than Whites, portrayed in TV commercials. When you take a hard look at that era, you will find that the general idea of those in charge was to conform to the socially acceptable norms for that period and never bothering to take into consideration the enormous amount of talent being passed up/ignored simply because God, being nondiscriminatory in His gift giving, just happened to place the ingenuity for the solution to cancer, for instance, in the body of a person who didn't fit in your self-scripted model of social norms. Consequently, the results of your particular racism would most assuredly cause millions of lives to be lost earlier than was needed to say nothing of the trillions of dollars lost in the process.

It's a fact that racism thrives because those in power (mostly Whites) prosper greatly on the fears of the masses who, for the most part, would not dare to rock the boat and cause an upset to the acceptable norms.

Well, I got news for you: Important and substantive change never comes about without a measure of discomfort and suffering.

The change from law to grace came only after Jesus died on the cross of Calvary and rose on the third day. The freedoms we enjoy in these United States of America were only obtained after a bloody war with the British, and let's not forget the fact that many people gave their lives in a fight for the civil liberties of the Black man during the famous civil war, which I might add, some of our US citizens still find it acceptable to keep fanning winds of iniquity with such gross lies as there being a superior and an inferior race of people. How can any rational human believe such a lie when all known history traces the human race back to only one source? (The area around the Euphrates and Tigris rivers is commonly known as the area where man first evolved, if you will.)

The limited freedoms Blacks and other so-called race minorities enjoy were achieved only after the deaths of many individuals of all so-called races made sacrifices with their lives. And let's not forget the tremendous sacrifices our people of color made with their bodies as they were raped, castrated, and tortured at the hands of the Whites, who assiduously taught both of the dominate races that Blacks and any race other than the White race were born inferior to the White race.

What's really scary is the fact that most of this hate-filled teaching was done in the very churches that purported to be filled with the Holy Spirit.

Only in the last twenty years have we seen very large changes in the social norms of the so-called races. I would be negligent in this writing, not to mention the fact that when a righteous wave of changes evolves in our society, there is always a tide of unrighteous changes that get attached to the prevailing wave of changes and those who represent these add-on items and issues will swear by Peter, Paul, and Mary that their agenda was always in the midst of the original efforts of change proposal. Let me make this point very clear; Reverend Dr. Martin Luther King and the civil rights movement fought for equal treatment of all people. Our fight was primarily one that dealt with the extreme racial prejudice as it was manifested in the southern parts of the United States, where narrow-mindedness and reckless disregard for the life and liberties of racial minorities were commonplace.

I am aware that some will read this account and will proclaim that the many marches were for reasons other than civil rights. The march rallies I attended in Montgomery were strickly focused on freeing up civil rights for all people.

Some key elements that were essential to our corporate civil rights fight

Before we venture into our major struggle for Black equality at J&L Steel, we thought it necessary to list a few of the key elements that happened to be very essential to the success of our (the J&L Black Caucus) efforts during this very tumultuous time.

1. *Self-examination*

In order to get the job done, one must start with a true assessment of themselves. Because of the colossal task ahead, the first thing needed is for one to have an introspective view of self. Whenever one is intent on changing a person, nation, society, culture, etc., one needs to take into account and ask, What are my goals or objective that would finish this project, and how will I reach said goals?

2. *Learn how to discern while knowing your limitations.*

True discernment does not come from your own intellect, but rather it is laced with God's omniscience, for *God only have infinite wisdom, knowledge, and understanding.*

3. *Acknowledge the difficulty and pray.*

The road to freedom and justice is never smooth but is attainable by engaging the power of the Holy Spirit through prayer.

4. *Understand the need for a strong Holy Spirit connection.*

During these tremendous corporate battles, few could be trusted to carry the mantle of leadership because such battles could only have a positive outcome if the one taking charge was endowed with a tenacious spirit, was *unselfish*, and *courageous* while *being careful*. Most of all, one needed to be *led by the Holy Spirit*, which would necessitate a serious prayerful life while keeping your life in such a way that God the Father, the Son, and the Holy Ghost will hear your fainted cry and answer your plea for help. Such person would do well to remember what Isaiah said:

> But your iniquities have separated between
> you and your God, and your sins have hid his
> face from you, that he will not hear. (Isaiah 59:2
> KJV)

5. *Divest yourself of any selfish motive for making the challenge*

Selfish motives are easily detected by your corporate opponents (that's exactly what they will be looking for when you challenge) and will serve to discredit, disenfranchise, and otherwise derail your entire effort. Remember, the people you are challenging are constantly looking for ways to shut you down without subjecting themselves to credible charges of provable retaliation in response to your inquiry into affirmative action as it is being applied by the corporate structure.

Up front (from the start of your efforts), you must have unselfish motives, and the primary reason is because whatever and whoever will be opposing you will almost always calculate their counter (to your position) using the supposition that your motives are more selfish rather than altruistic. During the early eighties, I was offered a very high position in the corporation with the stipulation that I would cease my inquiries into affirmative action as it relates to Blacks. I informed the official that I would most assuredly accept such a promotion, but my concerns for affirmative action as it relates to Blacks would continue until real and substantive changes were put in place on a corporative scale. You guessed it! I didn't get the very high position because I didn't agree to the sell-out terms that were (from the corporate perspective) the reason for the offer in the first place.

6. *Be ready to accept help from unusual sources*

As you advance and make your objectives known, you will encounter some who are on the privilege side of the ledger, who will surprise you by being in agreement with your stated objectives (which is equal opportunity for all). *Prayfully consider allowing them to help you achieve your noble objective.* One such individual (of Caucasian origin), because of his position in the corporation, actually provided evidence that we could not have otherwise obtained and that evidence was used to successfully argue our (the J&L Black Caucus) cases before a federal judge in the US court system.

7. *Fortunately, discrimination is usually very discernible. However, the benefactors are busy ignoring the evidence.*

For example, at our corporation, some of the vice presidents I conversed with didn't have a college degree, and yet the same individuals were requiring college degrees for any potential Black to be accepted as a management trainee. Not only that, but they hired some Blacks with college degrees and brought them in to fill clerical positions while allowing Whites to be promoted to management positions without the benefit of a college degree.

The reason race discrimination thrives so well and so long is because those who benefited from it ignored the moral decadence of the practice simply because it was a practice that they (Whites) benefited from. The troubling thing about this is that these are the same liberals who claim they wanted us free from slavery in the South. Being from South Alabama, I can truly attest to the fact that southern race discrimination was much more brutal and overt, nevertheless, Northern race discrimination represented its share of injustice also. I am reminded of the words from Reverend Dr. Martin Luther King: "Injustice anywhere is a threat to justice everywhere."

Consequently, we are called upon to do our part to conquer injustice wherever it raises its ugly head. At the time of this writing (2020), we are still waging major wars against racial injustice. The recent focus has been centered on police brutality. What's interesting is that the kind of brutality that were seen (via recordings) waged against Blacks is rarely inflicted on our White counterpart.

Things to remember (addressed to the Caucus)

Things to remember (addressed to the J&L Black Caucus at the end of the year 1980 by H. L. McNeil):

1. Conservatives, as it politically applied, means to keep in place status quo values. For Blacks, this viewpoint is disastrous because we cannot afford stagnation; we must move forward.
2. It can be done; it will be done when you take the necessary steps to make it happen.
3. Mankind, by nature, favors those people whose human attributes are most like their own.

4. Gaining acceptability by those you work with is usually desirable. However, the price paid for this privilege is often too high.
5. *Compromise* is often used as the key word by individuals trying to reach reasonable solutions to various problems. One should be careful not to compromise basic principles in such endeavors.
6. The degree of effectiveness for the J&L Black Caucus will be predicated on God's grace and your participation.
7. Saving face to corporate officials is sometimes more important than losses on the profit and loss statement.
8. Black folks, where jobs are concerned, can ill afford such luxurious emotions as enviousness and jealousness. Such tools have been used against us for much too long.
9. There will be those who will rise and show measures of success. However, if such upward mobility is to continue, your moral support is needed, even if the recipient does not want it, or feels it is unnecessary. Be proud of the success of your fellow person.
10. No matter what you think of the Black person who is, for the time, a measure above you on the corporate success ladder, you can be sure that he or she is less apt to racially discriminate against you than a White counterpart.
11. Racism is with us today. Ignoring it will not make it go away. If you doubt me, then you are not listening to anybody's news.
12. It is counterproductive to harbor racist thoughts. However, do not be blind to actuality.
13. None, not even Black folks, will get 100 percent participation in any endeavor.
14. The average exempt salary is approximately $30,000–$35,000 per year (in the early 1980s). Where do you fit in?
15. Do you believe J&L is an equal opportunity employer?

Introduction to J&L Steel

As I indicated elsewhere, in 1964, when I graduated from Camden Academy High School, because I attended college, I was able to receive an educational deferment from the military draft system that existed in those days.

I graduated from Alabama State University in January of 1969, and J&L Steel (a Fortune 500 company) recruited me to go to work for them as a financial management trainee.

Anyway, I accepted the invitation and began a career in financial management at this particular company. I got my unwanted US Army invitation in the summer of 1969, with orders to report for duty soon thereafter.

Later conversations with some anonymous but not-so-anonymous company official, I found out that Fortune 500 companies that had substantial US government contracts were told by President Lynden B. Johnson that if they wanted to keep their contracts, they would have to hire some minorities. *(At that particular time, "minorities" was a reference to Blacks or Negroes. But soon after, the definition was changed to include White women. I am always astonished at those people who claim race discrimination can be solved by the inclusion of members of the offending race responsible for the discrimination in the first place! Is it any wonder why, upon review, this setting was in 1969 and today, 2023, or fifty-four years later, we are still wrestling with the same problem.)* I digressed. As I was saying, the president of the United States of America made hiring some minorities in the management sectors of the corporate structure a kind of mandate, if you will. They could no longer be limited to mere clerical and not be included in management.

These changes resulted in me being the first Black financial management trainee to be hired, and about the same time, J&L hired a fellow Black management trainee in personnel name Bill Cook, who became a friend of mine. There were a few others in various management disciplines.

Returning from the war

After serving and being release honorably from the military in July of 1971, I returned to my job at J&L Steel. The federal government in those days required companies to reinstate former employees who had been drafted by the military.

My first assignment was at the Gateway 3 Towers in downtown Pittsburgh, Pennsylvania, and as a financial management trainee, I reported directly to the vice president of finance, Mr. J. R. Fleming, a very nice and truly remarkable man of seemly intense passion for the underprivileged or those underrepresented. I will briefly share with you what brought me to this conclusion about this man. Mr. Fleming assigned me to work as a financial management trainee under the temporary supervision of the Aliquippa control center supervisor. Somehow, while talking to some of the employees at the center, I was asked what my salary was. I quickly volunteered the information, and I soon noticed a distinct unfriendly change in the attitude of most of the surrounding employees that worked at this center, including that of the supervisor.

At the close of the day, I received a call from VP Fleming, asking me to report to his office in downtown Pittsburgh, Pennsylvania the next morning. So I finished out my day at the control center in Aliquippa and reported to Mr. Fleming's office the next morning.

The vice president greeted me with his usually nice smile and then asked me how things were going down at Aliquippa. I let him know that everyone treated me with expected cordiality, and after asking me if I wanted a cup of coffee, he then got down to the business of why he had called me into the headquarters.

He started by saying, "I have two concerns that have been brought to my attention" by some of our staff here in headquarters and those in service at the control center at Aliquippa.

1. He informed me that the girls, as he (being very old school) referred to the female clerks working on the floor at our headquarters office (in those days, there were extremely few, if any, females of color working in management posi-

tions), the female clerks, complained to him about the fact that when I would talk or address them, they notice that I would never look them in the face while talking, but instead I would look down or to the left or the right of them while they were trying to have a conversation with me. To wit, I explained to him that for the last twenty-two years of my life, which was all my life, to look a White woman in the face was a potential capital offense. This particular fact was true since until 1965, the state laws were not designed to protect us but to enslave us. I further explained that until 1965, I was not a full human being, according to the Alabama State law. I then explained that since what I did by not looking at the White women in the office was an act of self-preservation, it would be very difficult to reverse this course of behavior now that I happened to be in a state that recognized me as human and thus would have some possible redress to such draconian socially legislative order that I referred to above.

Mr. Fleming stated that he had forgotten that I was brought up in the Old South, and he said that he understood the situation and further said the matter needed no further attention.

2.   As for the second concern, he was clearly more bewildered. He said that he had been informed that I had given out the amount of salary that I was being paid to those who asked and further said that my actions had caused a great uproar at the Aliquippa control center, especially since my management trainee salary was higher than even the control center supervisor's salary at that time.

Again, I had to enlighten Mr. Fleming that I was brought up in an agricultural environment and had absolutely no experience in what protocols existed in office life. I explained that this particular experience was my first exposure to being in the surrounding of an office. I let him know that there were business offices in the area I grew up in, but Negroes were never afforded the privilege to work at such places, and consequently, I couldn't have known that telling one's salary was a violation of standard office protocol.

Again, he said that he understood the situation and said the matter needed no further attention. However, he did make me aware of the subject protocol and various other office protocols, to wit I thanked him, and the matter was consequently closed.

After my financial management trainee period of about one year ended, I was assigned to the internal audit department as a junior internal auditor. In this department, I happened to come into contact with some very nice coworkers and some not too nice people. My manager was a very old-school gentleman in his late sixties or seventies. Anyway, he treated me as fair as he could except the one time all my coworkers and I felt that he crossed the line of racism.

We were having a meeting where the boss was giving us some pointers on how to recognize some improprieties when out in the field during an audit (I really don't remember the exact conversation that led him to say this very inappropriate and vile statement), he said something like the following: Whenever you see a situation where the books are unbalanced, there is "a nigger in the woodpile somewhere." There were about eight auditors in the room, and all heads turned to me and looked with intense shame (or so I thought) about the fact that our boss had the nerve and unmitigated gall to use such language in the presence of a Black person. Every one of them apologized profusely for the boss's uncouth behavior. However, what this incident told me is that he was using the language that he had become accustomed to while talking to his staff. Perhaps the real problem was, *they only thought it wrong to use such language in front of one of the persons such language was designed to demean.* In other words, it's ok to debase an entire class/race of people but just don't let them hear you doing it. That is precisely how *systemic racism* gets so entrenched into our society.

The statement came out of his mouth so smoothly that I am certain he didn't realize that it was inappropriate, and maybe I am giving him too much credit. In any case, given my background (from

Alabama), I was all too familiar with White folk feeling that Blacks were to be the object of their scorn.

However, we moved on from there, and as you might have guessed, there were way too many instances of racial tension, uncomfortable situations, and the like. We all know that four hundred years of overt and systematic racial discrimination can't be put to rest in a short period of time. However, as Reverend Dr. Martin Luther King use to say, If you are the one being oppressed, the time for relief is *now*!

I have often wondered if those evangelicals of the 1960s, who stood so solidly against racial equality/integration, actually believed in some of the intense and inaccurate spiritual dogma that often came out of their mouths. I wonder if those who have not been the object of systemic racism think that such oppression is beneficial to our great republic. Do they not know that together we stand, and divided we fall?

(Update to January 16, 2021) The president of the United States, Mr. Donald Trump, was impeached a second time by a majority lead democratic congress. This was done because of the fact that this president had worked so very heard to and did convince his base, an extremely conservative base, that the recent elections, should he not win, would be a definite indication that the election had been stolen. This he alleged, even after his lawyers filed over fifty cases with various state, federal, and the supreme US courts, and they were all were thrown out for lack of evidence.

His various speeches and hate-filled rhetoric led to a January 6 insurrection on the United State Capitol, and in the aftermath, it was found that these extreme "right wingers" had plans to execute and/or hold hostage the vice president because the president had publicly requested the republican vice president Mike Pence to ignore the law and not certify the recent election results. What is interesting about this is that the political experts and law professors had declared that Mr. Pence's actions could, in no way, nullify the election results. There is also evidence they were planning to kill some of the political folks at the capitol.

Let's face it—those who have participated in systematic oppression while simultaneously benefitting from four hundred years of racial entitlements find it extremely difficult to give up those systemic and unjust ways of during things. In other words, the insurrection might have had great success a century ago but not today. Mr. Trump and his base learned a valuable lesson on that day, and that lesson is, What was good for reconstruction and other dark times in our democratic past is no longer effective in today's society for several reasons. *One*, our society is more diversified and not just composed of Black or White folks. *Two*, the violent ways of the extreme right of our society are no longer the prevailing method we use to regulate or control, if you will, our society. *Three*, our society no longer believes that public floggings, hangings, or lynching are to be used for one part of our society to lord over another part, no matter what is alleged by demigods, such as Mr. Donald Trump.

Inequities noted and challenged

One of the things that was quite obvious about the corporate world at J&L (Jones and Laughlin Steel, later to become LTV Steel) was the fact that until I and other similar situated Blacks began showing up in 1969, Blacks had been systematically excluded from any meaningful role in management at this, and many other companies scattered across the country. In my role as a financial management trainee, I had the opportunity to observed Black participation or the lack thereof in many of our corporate offices and various subdivisions, and almost everywhere I travel, I was the only Black in an exempt or management type positions. The picture was very bleak from my perspective; however, if you are sitting on the privileged side of the coin, I suppose it would seem as so many have said: "We just can't find a good candidate for hire."

One day, while I was together with a number of my Black friends and coworkers, all of whom were clerical with maybe one exception, we began to reflect on the fact that our company was severely lacking in minority representation in the exempt/management ranks. At this particular time (about 1977), the audit department was situated at what was known as the plaza. Now, as we began to think about what the numbers were and what wasn't.

First approach too slow

Anyway, doing the latter part of 1977, I began making individual contact with some of the J&L upper echelon, such as Mr. John Purser, VP of public affairs, and this particular individual seemed to have a concern for this obvious, contagious, and systematic corporate injustice of racial inequality. Having said all that, I am not sure of Mr. Purser's motive; however, I must say he was instrumental in arranging some key meetings with some other vice presidents, who subsequently gave lip service, and to be fair about it, they did make a few steps in the right directions.

I assume that Mr. Purser saw this situation as part of his job since the unequal employment opportunities I was alleging had the potential for ominous public relations for the entire corporate community status.

Mr. Purser held an extensive one-on-one meeting with me on January 25, 1978, where I shared with him some clear and concise examples of unequal opportunity practices that I had observed right under his nose and in his own corporate surroundings.

Pre-exile efforts

During the year 1978, I was a part of, at least, eight high-level meetings with J&L VPs and managers. In these meetings, my goal was to try to convince these individuals of the necessity to put in place company policies that would actually lead to real equal opportunity for Blacks in our workplace. I wrote several follow-up letters to these individuals, detailing the oral conversations that we had engaged in. Eventually, I came to the inevitable conclusion that these individuals didn't mind talking about affirmative action as it related to Blacks, but they lacked the will to challenge the status quo and, thus, bring real affirmative change to our corporate structure that would benefit our Black employees. Below, I list some on the meetings:

1. January 25, 1978—Extensive talks with vice president of publicity, John Purser, who spoke on how the corporate structure might benefit from suggestions from concerned employees such as me.
2. January 30, 1978—Brief talk with Mr. Purser about the same subject
3. February 13, 1978, at the Pittsburgh Press Club—Met with vice president of industrial relations, John Kirkwood, and vice president of publicity, John Purser. At this meeting, these gentlemen requested that I submit suggestions to them revealing, how I perceived J&L might improve in areas of equal opportunity as it relates to Blacks. They also suggested that I could possibly submit some résumés of qualified Blacks to them for their consideration.
4. April 30, 1978—I sent a follow up letter to Mr. Kirkwood, thanking him for allowing me to express my views and letting him know that since our meeting, I had talked about affirmative action and "affirmative attitudes" with several members of J&L's personnel department. I explained to Mr. Kirkwood that my overriding concern pertained to the low numbers of Blacks in J&L's affirmative action numbers. This point was important because of the corporate tendency to fill most of their EEOC requirements with White women. I explained to Mr. Kirkwood that I didn't see how filling the quotas/target/goals with White women would be an improvement to my overriding concerns about Blacks not having equal opportunity at the workplace.

In this April 30, 1978, letter, I did what was suggested of me by submitting eight suggestions for constructive change. I will not bother to list them all. However, I will talk briefly about two of the suggestions I made. (a) I suggested that they should consider hiring a conscientious Black for the purpose of recruiting salaried exempt and nonexempt prospective employees, explaining that this act would be a frank acknowledgment of the subjective element involved in the hiring process, allowing the interviewer and the interviewee to relate to one another on a very general basis. (b) Let J&L's affirmative action records be an open book, ready for review upon request by interested individuals within J&L and affiliated organizations.

Also, I made a point of clarity because a member of the personnel department expressed reservations about my intentions and appeared to have interpreted my inquiry about affirmative action as something less than honorable. I assured this VP that my efforts should not be viewed as threatening, but rather they should be seen as an attempt to help the corporation achieve its stated goal of equal opportunity for all sectors of our great corporation.

I acknowledge that the personnel department had asked me to visit some college campuses.

5. May 9, 1978—Sent a letter to J. T. Delmore, director of corporate internal audit of LTV (the parent of J&L), my boss. I explained to him that the J&L personnel department had asked me to travel to Xavier University in New Orleans and Norfolk State College in Virginia on May 17 and 18 respectively to assist in promoting college relations for the J&L personnel department.

6. May 23, 1978—Sent letter to A. M. Griffin, general manager of personnel, explaining that I traveled on May 18, 1978, with Ms. Chris M. Infante, manager of employment to Norfolk State College (HBCU). I reported on our stated goals of recruiting and establishing better college relations. Two candidates were considered for further interviews at J&L's home location.

7. May 23, 1978—Sent a letter to A. M. Griffin, general manager personnel, explaining that I traveled to Xavier University on May 17, 1978, with Ms. Alanna Roberts, Pittsburgh works employment. The personnel department provided us with seven detailed suggestions on our stated goals of recruiting and establishing better college relations.

Exiled to Texas

8. Note that right after the above series of events/meeting, etc., I was sent in *exile* (no! the company officials didn't call it "exile"} to Houston, Texas, from June 19, 1978, through December 13, 1978. I remember the "powers that be," making some kind of excuse for me to be in Huston, Texas, at our pipe division to "fill in" for a person who had resigned from his position as inventory clerk, a position by its very title is clerical. Who has ever heard of an exempt salaried employee (management type) being sent across the country to work for six months in a clerical position? The problem with the excuse was that while my assignments were certainly their prerogative, no one else in the audit or any other department, for that matter, had ever been handed such an assignment. However, on September 1, 1978, John Delmore, the audit director, called me and asked me why I had attempted to set up a meeting with the vice president of personnel, Mr. Kirkwood. To wit, I reminded him that I had already informed him that I had been asked by Mr. Kirkwood to keep the lines of communication open between us. Previously, I had asked Mr. Delmore if he wanted me to spend my vacation time and my money toward this effort. I reminded him of his retort: He said, *"Any problem with affirmative action in J&L is also a problem for L.T.V. Therefore, continue to do as they asked you to."*

9. Nevertheless, on October 17, 1978, I sent a four-page single-spaced letter to John Delmore with the subject: "Report of My Inquiry about Affirmative Action as it Relates of Blacks." In this letter was a twelve-point synopsis of my efforts to help J&L achieve equal employment opportunity for all. Below, I have listed most of these points in an even more abbreviated form:

    a. February 21, 1978—Met with Mr. Wayne Holt of the Urban League in an effort to seek qualified Blacks for possible employment and reported to Mr. A. M. Griffin the same day.

b.   Mr. Griffin asked that the lines of communication be open between us. I submitted five résumés to Mr. Griffin, and he suggested that I meet with the manager of employment services, Mr. C. D. Engle and Ms. C. M. Infante.

c.   In a March 1, 1978, meeting with Mr. Engle and Ms. Infante, they explained that J&L affirmative action applied to all minorities, not just Blacks. I explained that the program apparently excluded Blacks entirely in the exempt administrative capacity at J&L's headquarters since there had been no increase in the number of Blacks working in this area during my entire tenure of nine years.

d.   In a March 8, 1978, informal meeting with Ms. Infante and Mr. Griffin, I explained that I was constructing a letter to the vice president of personnel, putting forth my thoughts and recommendations for clarity's sake.

e.   May 10, 1978—met with Plaza personnel development and service representative, Mr. John Drotos. The Plaza was a large, flat one-story building, with approximately 250 employees. (Oh, by the way, the Plaza didn't have any exempt Black J&Lers.) I met with Mr. Drotos at the request of his boss, Mr. Griffin. I noted that the Blacks that had college degrees in the Plaza were all clerical [nonexempt], but many of their White contemporaries, with and without college degrees, were given exempt jobs.

f.   In a June 6, 1978, conversation with two Plaza personnel representatives, three concerns were mentioned as reflected below:

Blacks having a bachelor's degree or above noticed a trend of non-Blacks being able to get promoted from a nonexempt status to an exempt status without the benefit of a bachelor's degree when in fact there were qualified Blacks with college degrees being overlooked.

Blacks have not been allowed to work at all in salary payroll because some well-meaning individuals felt that having a Black in this area would easily expose the company to scrutiny by outside Black-oriented antidiscrimination organizations.

To summarize the June to December exile situation, I suppose "the powers that be" thought that sending me in exile to Huston, Texas, would somehow cause me to stop my inquiry into J&L affirmative action concerns. I stayed at an opulence apartment, usually reserved for higher echelon guests. The apartment building was rumored to be the home of eighteen millionaires. I don't know how true the rumor was, but my clothes were washed or dry cleaned daily. The apartment kitchen was fully stocked with every modern appliance. The apartment was cleaned daily, and I never saw a bill for the apartment or the services rendered. And though I was working in a job that was likely paying at lower rate than my salary, the "powers that be" never lowered my pay rate.

Nevertheless, none of these eccentric accoutrements could have and never would have had any prevailing effect on me as I continued to concentrate on the focus matter, which was affirmative action or the lack thereof as relating to Blacks primarily in the administrative sector of J&L Steel Corporation. You see, I really didn't feel that I had anything to lose. Think about it for a moment; here I was, working in a relatively low-level management job after nine years of employment. I had a bachelor's in business administration from college. The amount of money I was making could have been earned in many sectors of our great society. The point I am making is simple, if a man is fighting for a justifiable cause, then it should be honored. If one is "troubling the waters gratuitously" then prove it and fire him.

Their problem centered on the fact that before the exile, they (the vice president of personnel) not only didn't deny that my assertions/accusations were factual, but the personnel department actually had me submit résumés to them and, as noted above, this department sent me to help with recruiting by traveling to Xavier University in New Orleans and Norfolk State College in Virginia.

Interestingly enough how, in May of 1978, these corporate executives were pretending to enlist my help in solving an apparent affirmative action problem as it relates to Blacks, but when I returned to Pittsburgh, I apparently was perceived as the problem, and somehow, "the powers that be" determined that I could best be silenced by being sent to Huston Texas for about a half year.

I wonder how long they would have kept me assigned in Huston had I not demonstrated my ability to use the phone to call the vice president of personnel to honor his request that we keep the lines of communication open? Anyway, I came back to Pittsburgh in December, and the "powers that be" knew the fight was not yet over.

Postexile fight

Somehow, we got some figures from the human relations department that showed approximately a slight increase in Black folks working at the satellite semiheadquarters location that had the strange resemblance to the navy aircraft carrier. This building was much easier to get to because instead of being located in the downtown area, where very hectic traffic and parking conditions existed, this area had plenty of parking, was right across the river from the downtown area, and had all the amenities of the building where we used to be (which was the Gateway 3 building) but without the downtown congestion and the devastating daily traffic jams.

February 1, 1979, Mr. Dutch Lodewyks, the acting vice president of finance for J&L, called my boss (the audit manager) and instructed him to have me report to his office in the Plaza at 5:15 p.m.

My boss said he hadn't been briefed on what the meeting would be about. There was a sort of situation that surrounded being called in to a vice president's office at or around 4:30 p.m. or after in the Plaza, where my office was situated. Usually, it meant that you would be receiving parting instructions from the company (i.e., getting fired). As a consequence of this type of thinking, I called my wife (Leslie) before going into Mr. Lodewyks' office to let her know that as a result of my affirmative action activities, I would be given a notice of job termination at this upcoming 5:15 p.m. meeting. She said she understood.

So I gathered up a few nerves, and I would have prayed before entering his office (which I did a lot of during those challenging days.).

Anyway, I showed up at exactly 5:15 p.m. and came into his office visibly shaken and somewhat unnerved. (For you see, like the Hebrew boys in the fiery furnace—Daniel in the lion's den, Jonathan against the Philistines, and so many others in scripture—I knew that the Lord *could* rescue me from any situation, but I didn't know that he *would* in this particular situation.) I was certain that God would eventually bring His desired divine will into action one way or another. There was no doubt about that, but I didn't know exactly how this part of the situation would be dealt with.

As I said before, at 5:15 p.m., I reported to Mr. Lodewyks' Plaza office and of course was very nervous. Mr. Lodewyks recognized how I felt and said, "Be at ease. I am not going to fire you!" Then he said, "Relax. I want to explain something to you." He said he had read my recent letter (*probably the October 17, 1978, letter to Mr. John Delmore, director of LTV auditing, where I was working at that time*). In this letter, I exposed at least six points where J&L was severely deficient in the way they treated Blacks when compared to White employees. Below, I will reiterate these points:

1. In the plaza area, Blacks with college degrees were given nonexempt (or clerical) jobs, while Whites with the same qualifications were slotted into exempt (management) positions.

2. It appeared that some thought/review should be given to situations where Blacks, who inquired about a desire to advance were subsequently receiving lower evaluations, which might be retaliation for daring to question the boss's promotion standards.

3. It appeared that J&L had improved its recruiting program. The apparent problem, over the years, has been one of hiring Blacks after they were invited in for interviews.

4. Black in the Plaza, particularly those with bachelor's degrees and above, were concerned with the trend of non-Blacks being able to get promoted from a nonexempt status to exempt status without the benefit of a bachelor's degree when the same standard is not applied to Blacks.

5. It appears that some well-meaning individuals felt that having a Black in salary payroll would easily expose the company to scrutiny by outside Black-oriented, antidiscrimination organizations, and consequently, Blacks were not allowed to work in that department.

6. It should be noted that as of February 1, 1979, the Plaza employed more than one hundred exempt employees, but not one of them were Black.

This February 1, 1979, letter concluded with the following statement: "We say that we (J&L) are an equal opportunity employer. With this slogan in mind, headquarters would be a good place to exemplify such affirmation of commitment. I believe that there are qualified Blacks able to fill jobs at all levels at J&L's headquarters."

So now I was sitting, and Mr. Lodewyks said he had read my letter and, at first, was quite upset and determined that if he found any statement on the letter to be unfounded or untrue, he would be sure to fire me.

Then he began to go through the letter point by point. He elaborated by saying that he actually made inquiries as to the authenticity and validity of each claim I made in the letter. Then he said that he wasn't able to debunk a single statement in the letter. And suddenly, he surprised me by reaching into his desk drawer and pulling out forty-two slips of paper that represented forty-two persons whom he had selected (but hadn't given notice) to be new employees at the Plaza location. Then he said, of the forty-two potential new hires, only one was of Black decent, and that person was being brought in to fill the lowest position of all the other forty-one White potential new hires. Then Mr. Lodewyks said, "This is why I sent for you to come to my office. I want you to witness this yourself." He then took the forty-two slips of paper and tore them up, and he said he really didn't know or hadn't paid attention to the fact that the entire exempt salaried staff at the Plaza consisted of all White employee and said, "Even though I didn't intentionally overlook Blacks for the exempt (management) positions, I made no great effort to find any either."

I thought it a bit odd that Mr. Lodewyks was saying this in light of the fact that just seven months earlier, on May 17 and 18 of 1978, I had been on a recruiting trip to Xavier University and Norfolk State University respectively with representatives of the corporate personnel department for the expressed purpose of finding qualified Black candidates for positions in J&L.

Since none of the candidates we interviewed were offered jobs at J&L, nor were any of them, to my knowledge, ever considered for a position, exempt or otherwise, at J&L, I was bewildered when I heard the often 1970s and 1980s refrain: "We can't find a good one." This was a statement often used in the corporate circles to suggest that qualified Blacks just didn't exist for our corporate positions.

And many in personnel would say, "We have looked but just couldn't find any qualified African Americans (as we were sometimes called in those days) to fit in the jobs we have to offer." Anyway, getting back to Mr. Lodewyks, he said that he would be actively seeking qualified Blacks to fill these jobs, and I believed he did his best to see that some of the jobs that were represented in those forty-two slips of paper were filled by Black candidates. After our meeting, there were at least two exempt Black personnel hired, and a number of nonexempt (clerical) jobs were filled by Black men and women. I believe this man did the best he could in the extremely status quo–regimented hierarchy he was working in.

The 1978–79 figures indicated that Blacks working in management at this particular location was scarce as hen's teeth, and there were absolutely no Blacks in management out of all the people employed and working at this particular location with the exception made by Mr. Lodewyks as indicated above. And so, we (the Blacks at J&L Steel Corporation) on September 30, 1980, decided to form a group that would put forth an intelligent and meaningful challenge to these racial inequalities.

There were several people who were at the forefront of the formation of the ensuing group of approximately ninety challengers. Oh, by the way, we actually had an executive committee that was really instrumental in putting forth an intelligent challenge to the established corporate structure. My right-hand man and vice president, *Elmer* Patterson, also a vice president, *Lorraine* Williams. The other part of the inner circle of decisions makers were *Joanne* Broadus, who was treasurer; *Sandra* Ford; *Don* Harper; *Beatrice* Hogan; *Gwen* Howze; *Alex* and *Anna* Jones; *Charles* Lemon; *Stephanie* Phillips; *Augusto* Protho; *Jim* Stowers; *Ed* Weatherly; *Thomas* Bigelow; *Frank* Boyd; *Gwen* Foster; *George* Joy; *Betty* Knight; and *James* Madison. At the forefront of all my important decisions was *Jesus Christ*. Some of you reading this might say "Not so" because of my earned reputation as a frequent and almost daily heavy drinker. However, those who were close to me knew that when the Caucus faced a crisis with the company, I would always go on a six month or one year refrain from drinking any alcoholic beverages and would be intermittingly fasting for days in between these intervals. The twenty-one individuals mentioned above were heavily involved in the many J&L Black Caucus decisions.

The group organized by establishing a constitution and bylaws that would be used to guide us and keep good order. We established certain dues in order to be able to have the resources to make our presence known to our company, J&L Steel, and the general public. We made no apologizes for seeking and receiving help from Mr. Bob Pitts and the local NAACP.

We elected officers and set up a bank account at the local Black bank in Pittsburgh. Various public people were invited to speak to us, including Mr. Mel Good, the first Black national news correspondent. (He was the uncle of one of our members, Stephanie Phillips.) We retained lawyers to help us with establishing our group as a 501(c)(3) nonprofit organization.

Reignite the fight

Being from rural Alabama, I was very familiar with the types of things that the "powers that be" (as Alabama governor George Wallace used to say) would maneuver when faced with what they considered a somewhat uppity Negro. Their first mode of attack was usually made by enlisting the help of an informant, as the Northerners referred to them. However, in the Old South, we Blacks referred to them as Uncle Toms. Now let me explain to you as Carter G. Woodson implied in his book *The Mis-Education of the Negro*, these kinds of colored individual don't have to be shown the back door for entry into a house. They will look for it, and if they can't find one, they will cut one out for their own entry, for they have been trained that way.

Report to my fellow employees

Realizing that my efforts to address affirmative action as it relates to Blacks was primarily being hampered by the status quo corporate White officials, I wrote the following June 16, 1980, letter to all of my fellow (Black) employees:

Dear Fellow Employees:
This writing is to serve notice that I have been trying for more than two years to plead with Jones and Laughlin to properly include Blacks in their Affirmative Action Plan.

My inquiry into this matter was prompted by the fact that during my tenure in the J&L working environment, I have seen a trend of an absolute exclusionary policy, where Blacks are concerned, in any meaningful jobs in J&L Steel.

During the last two years, some good efforts were made by the accounting department, though hardly enough to warrant major accommodations.

For those who may not be familiar with the situation, let me give you a synopsis of the developments:
In a February 13, 1978, meeting with Mr. John Kirkwood, vice president of industrial relations, and Mr. John Purser, vice pres-

ident of public relations, I expressed my alarming concern about an apparent trend of J&L's policy of excluding Blacks in their hiring and promotion practices. This trend was visible in exempt and nonexempt administrative positions. During this two-hour luncheon, Mr. Kirkwood admitted J&L's shortcomings in the exempt administrative area and asked for suggestions as to how to do a better job in the area of Affirmative Action as it relates to Blacks. He also asked me to submit résumés of qualified applicants to the Personnel Department. He said he would attempt to review them personally.

Finally, after so many attempts to get J&L Steel management interested in our (the J&L Black Caucus) mission of equal opportunity for all of company's employees, we decided to work with the local NAACP located in the Hill District to help us move the issue to the ears of the public via a press conference we scheduled to take place on August 19, 1981, at 10:00 a.m. at the NAACP headquarters in the Hill District.

As I have indicated elsewhere, whenever I was faced with what I determined was a somewhat insurmountable situation or set of obstacles, I would start either a *half* or a *whole* year break from drinking alcoholic beverages for at least two reasons: (1) I needed a clear and clean line of communication between myself and God. David said, "Order my steps in thy word: and let not any iniquity have dominion over me" (Psalm 119:133 KJV). And since I tended to overindulge, I decided that during these trying times, I would abstain from its use totally and thus avoid the iniquity of alcohol overindulgence. (2) Also, during this same period of a *half* or a *whole*, year I would often have days of fasting, where I would not drink nor eat anything in an effort to get a real closeness to Jesus Christ. As the quote from the song "Amazing Grace" indicates, *"Through many dangers toils and snares I have come. It was grace that brought me safe thus far and grace will lead me on."*

I remember a meeting with two vice presidents at the prestigious Duquesne Club. Of course, the first thing they offered to get for me as their guest was a drink, which I refused because (1) I was fasting, and (2) it's a fact that strong drinks dull the senses, and I wasn't so much concerned about their mental state as I was about mine.

The one thing I wanted both of these gentlemen to know is that I was there strictly for business and didn't need anything taking away the wisdom God had so graciously endowed me with.

Forced to take it public via press conference

As I indicated above, the Caucus held a press conference on Wednesday at 10:00 a.m., August 19, 1981, at the NAACP office in the Hill District. At the time of this press conference, the Hill District was known as the rough side of town, and it was at least 99 percent populated with Black folks. I make the foregoing note because, as of this writing (2023), the real estate picture has been reversed, and the Hill District has become an area of very expensive houses and the affluents are now well situated in this part of town.

And so, on the day of our press conference, all the most inner circle of the Caucus took vacation days off work so that they could be in support of the press conference. Bear in mind that none of our Caucus members had any expertise in setting up a press conference; consequently, Mr. Pitts and his NAACP staff were extremely valuable to us doing this time of challenge. As a matter of fact, on the morning of the press conference, about half hour before the news media arrived, Mr. Pitts received a call from a high-ranking member of J&L personnel department, and in this call, the J&L representative had the unmitigated gall and audacity to suggest that the NAACP should not support the J&L Black Caucus in their fight against unequal employment because J&L supported (via purchasing a table annually) the NAACP annual dinner. To wit, Mr. Bob Pitts began to launch a barrage of counter insults at the representative. I heard him say, "Do you think you can have control over who the NAACP supports or not support by just buying a few tickets to a dinner once a year? Are you crazy?" Then he launched an onslaught of insults that were somewhat ugly, if you know what I mean.

All three of the major news press came. I was designated by the Caucus to be the official spokesperson for the group. I delivered the following Caucus-prepared press release to each of the News outlets that were represented.

Press Release, August 19, 1981

The J&L Black Caucus has called this press conference because we feel it is time that the public should be made aware of Jones and Laughlin Steel Corporation's refusal to sit down with its employees and work out solutions to the problems of the lack of equal opportunity as it relates to Black salaried employees in the corporation. We would like to state that the formation of the J&L Black Caucus in no way represents an attempt to establish a bargaining unit.

After repeated attempts to address the problem of unequal opportunity internally have failed, the J&L Black Caucus realizes we have no other recourse but to address this problem externally. In addition, we have the understanding that the problem of unequal opportunity within J&L cannot be considered as strictly an internal problem but is one that affects the entire community.

Previous attempts to address this problem included letters to the president and chief executive officer in June and August of this year, requesting meeting at which we had hoped to pinpoint the following problem areas and offer our viable solutions to them.

1. *J&L does not have, and has never had, a Black in the positions of vice president, nor are any Blacks presently placed in positions which would be considered as "training grounds" for these positions.*
2. *When Black college graduates are hired at J&L, it does not take them long to ascertain that there is virtually no opportunity for continuous career advancement, causing them to seek*

employment with corporations, which are less conservative in their treatment of Blacks.

3. *When Blacks within the corporation request promotions into supervisory or management positions, they are invariably refused and told to attain higher education. However, we have discovered numerous cases of White employees who are holding and being promoted into supervisory or management positions without having college degrees.*

Our only response to date from the president and chief executive officer was a letter from the general manager personnel, stating that he would not meet with the Caucus's chosen representatives and labeling our concerns regarding the lack of equal opportunity at J&L as unsubstantiated.

We would like to state at this point that we are still willing to meet with the president and chief executive officer, who is the only person in a position to institute corporate policy and ensure its compliance.

If, for some reason, the corporation feels that it cannot commit itself to the eradication of unequal opportunity, then we of the J&L Black Caucus will commit ourselves to exhausting any available and legal means to make equal opportunity a reality at J&L. *(End of press release for august 19, 1981.)*

Immediately after reading the above statement, representatives, including myself, answered questions from the news media about the nature of our organization and what possible fears we had about retribution from our beloved company officials. All of the media questions were answered in an honest and sincere manner; however, I remember one of the press members asking me why I wasn't personally fearful of losing my job at J&L. I explained to that reporter that fear has no rightful place in the halls of such a civil rights challenge as the one we had launched.

As I later reflected on the question, I remember how I really wanted to answer his question and held back because, after all, our chief goal was to engage in a peaceful and civil dialogue about how our company could or should live up to its various agreements labeled "consent decrees" (decrees or agreements entered into with government officials that spoke to nondiscriminatory treatment of said company employees) signed by top company official.

While I didn't answer the press during the interview, now I will answer the question of why I wasn't afraid of losing my job. *First*, one must remember my background and consider the environment I grew up in while living in Camden, Alabama, a town where I had lived all my life (some twenty years or so) and had never even heard of any person of color going to the polls to vote in our county (Wilcox). There might have been some who showed up, but they were never heard from again. It was a community where you frequently heard of lynching and various types of killings of people of color. My father and mother insisted that we never (even in a car) go out at night by ourselves. To show you how lawless this town was for Negroes, my first traffic ticket was given to me by a game warden who had no legal authority for such action except the fact that he was White and, as such, had the privilege to give the ticket, but only to Negroes. *Secondly*, being from an era, time, and place where my very life was always in jeopardy, the threat of losing a job pales in comparison to the threat of losing one's life. *Thirdly*, for the salary I was getting at the time, I could have found thirty or forty jobs in Pittsburgh, Pennsylvania that would pay as much or more. *Fourthly*, I learned from marching with Reverend Dr. Martin Luther King in the Selma to Montgomery march that when you face a challenge, such as trying to make a change in societal norms, one cannot go forward in fear, for he will most certainly fail.

Losing a low-paying exempt salaried job would be a small price to pay for a positive change in the corporate social construct that governed so many of the Black lives of that day and carried forward to future generations. What if Reverend Dr. Martin Luther King had operated his nonviolent movement in fear? I think you get the picture. You see, one of the benefits (if you can call it that) of having nothing or having little is that you don't really have much to lose, and yet there is so much to gain.

Certainly, one can understand why any group who has continually been shut out of the so-called better things of life would want to try to seek a better life, if not for themselves. Certainly, such persons would want a better life for their future generations.

Just think about it for a minute. Would you like to be held back for four or so generations and then told that you are now on your own but without the tools, money, housing etc. that your White counterparts have, yet you are expected to pull yourselves up by some really heavy-duty bootstraps?

I am always amazed when I think of those statements made by so many evangelicals back in the 1960s. Many of them said "the time for integrations is not now." What they were really saying was: If this equality thing must happen, please let it be after my lifetime. Oh! How selfish can our Christians brothers and sisters be?

When our secular society think on equality for Blacks and other minorities, I can fully understand why they are so resistant to give up their advantages. But what I don't understand is, why do you want to continue to keep a fifth or more of the population in neoslavery when so many atrocities (such as murder, rape, lynching) are associated with this type of republic?

Believe it or not, friends and neighbors, there is nothing righteous about rape, murder, lynching, unjustified arrest, beatings and treating your neighbor in an undignified manner. It might make you feel strong, but ultimately, such treatments divide our nation, which results in gross weakness for the entire republic, and that's not good for any of us.

Please know this: Blacks will never go back to being your slave, so get used to us demanding and loving our freedom just as much as you love yours.

ADDRESSING......questions by reporters at a new conference last week at NAACP headquarters, James McNeil, center, is flanked by two members of the Jones and Laughlin Steel Corporation's Black Caucus. (Mark Southers Photo).

J&L Blacks Charge Bias

Blacks who work for Jones and Laughlin Steel Corporation, are not afforded the same upper-echelon job opportunities as their white co-workers, says a group of Black J&L employees.

At a news conference at NAACP headquarters last week, members of the J&L Black Caucus accused the local company of discriminating against Blacks when it comes to promoting them to supervisory and upper management positions.

"Three tiers down from the presidency there are no Blacks, and we feel that it is not an ac-ident," said Henry McNeil, supervisor of J&L's Information Control Center, Hazelwood Works. "We have qualified and trained Blacks who can work in higher-echelon jobs within Jones and Laughlin," McNeil said.

The Black Caucus, which purports to have over 100 members, maintains that they have attempted on numerous occasions, to meet with Jones and Laughlin Steel Corporation's President Thomas Graham, to discuss their demands, but have been referred elsewhere.

To date, the only response the caucus says it has received is a letter from the general manager of personnel, D.L. Carroll, stating that he would meet with the caucus' chosen representatives, and labeling the concerns of the caucus regarding the lack of equal job opportunities at J&L as "unsubstantiated." At the news conference, Thomas Bigelow, a caucus member read from the June 15 letter; "Your letter (a previously submitted caucus letter) makes several unsubstantiated assertions including the blanket allegation that . . . equal opportunity has not yet become a reality in this corporation." The letter went on to say that two of the caucus' members have met with management and discussed their "personal problems." But McNeil insists that the caucus'

demands are not of a personal nature, but of a more systematic nature.

"We are not talking about personal problems," McNeil said, "we are talking about broad-based problem."

McNeil said the problem of unequal opportunity for Blacks at J&L must be solved from the top, because "the issues we're addressing include the vice-presidency.

"What we are trying to do is open up an avenue so that J&L begins to accept Blacks in the higher echelon positions of the corporation," McNeil said.

In May 1981, Jones and Lauglin Update, McNeil said J&L president Thomas Graham said he had "an open door policy" in discussing employee complaints. But McNeil said, "Apparently that open door policy does not apply to Black because he has refused to meet with us as a group, and our problems are not of a personal nature."

(Please turn to page 5)

Though J&L president Thomas Graham was not available for comment, William Gibbons, director of public relations for J&L, said management has made numerous attempts to meet with "representatives" of the Black Caucus, but has been unsuccessful.

"We have told representatives of the Black Caucus that we would like to meet with an individual who represents them, but they have refused," Gibbons said.

Asked what the Black Caucus plans to do if it continues to fail in attempts to meet with Graham, McNeil said "at this time we are not at liberty to discuss other courses of action we plan to take."

Specifically, the Jones and Laughlin Black Caucus asserts that:

J&L does not have, and never had, a Black in the positions of vice president, nor are any Blacks presently placed in positions which would be considered as "training grounds" for these positions.

When Black college graduates are hired at J&L, it does not take them long to ascertain that there is virtually no opportunity for continous career advancement, causing them to seek employment with corporations which are less conservative in their treatment of Blacks.

When Blacks within the Corporation request promotion promotions into supervisory or management positions, they are invariably refused and told to attain higher education. However, we have discovered numerous cases of white employees who are holding and being promoted into supervisory or management positions without having college degrees.

See the New Pittsburgh Courier, August 26, 1981, article, as it was published below.

End of the New Pittsburgh Courier, August 26, 1981, Article

After the press conference

On April 15, 1983, the J&L Black Caucus filed a form 990 with the IRS, requesting an exemption from income tax status 501(c)(3). On May 21, 1983, we received our tax-exempt status effective May 17, 1983.

Established an official nonprofit group

By this time, we realized that the struggle would be much longer and perhaps more difficult than we originally envisioned. Consequently, we drew up a set of rules and regulations with which to govern ourselves by. They were as follows:

Purpose:
To perpetuate the upward mobility of Blacks within Jones and Laughlin Steel Corporation.

Qualifications for membership:
Anyone interested in the perpetuation of the upward mobility of Blacks within Jones and Laughlin Steel Corporation

Preamble:
As responsible *name of organization* members of the Jones and Laughlin Steel Corporation, a subsidiary of the LTV Corporation, we hereby effect to better the working conditions and environments for all.

Voting:
Quorum—15 persons: 7 1/2 makes majority
Vote in May for officers' elections (to be held once a year)
Temporary—To change basic charter
        —Election of officers
        —Must have 1/3 of membership present for vote

Suggestion box:

Organization chart: to be included in the charter

Bylaws

How business is to be conducted:

1. Call to order
2. Reading of past minutes (including amendments to minutes report)
3. Old business
4. Committee reports
5. New business
6. Next meeting time and date

The executive director has discretion to precede committee reports for special business.

Official Preamble

Whereas: Jones and Laughlin's corporate commitment to affirmative action has produced negligible results on the situation of Blacks at J&L: and,

Whereas: Jones and Laughlin's voluntary consent decree has, in no meaningful way, had impact on the situation of Blacks at J&L, and it must be concluded that the EEOC, under the auspices of the federal government, is satisfied with paper compliance rather than demonstrable proof of qualitative improvement of the situation of minorities; and,

Whereas: Jones and Laughlin has limited its affirmative action commitment only to the inadequate EEOC framework and has made no viable attempt to reach beyond these guidelines to establish a more comprehensive corporate policy on equal opportunity: and

Whereas: It is empirically evident that Blacks are excluded from top-level management: and

Whereas: a commitment to equal opportunity on the part of major corporations is vital, not only in setting exemplary standards for smaller corporations and businesses but in a larger sense would aid in insuring domestic stability: and

Whereas: Repeated attempts to address the above issues on an individual level have resulted in very limited success, but no broad-base improvement in the situation of Blacks at J&L:

We therefore ordain to establish this organization with the specific purposes of:

A. Aiding Jones and Laughlin Steel Corporation in establishing a corporate policy, which truly exemplifies the principles of equal opportunity;

B. Eliminating job biases as they affect Blacks at J&L; and

C. Promoting the inclusion of Blacks in top-level management positions, i.e., MEC (management executive committee).

Actually, we had already started having monthly meetings, and we also collaborated with the local chapter of the NAACP, which was headed by Mr. Bob Pitts at that particular time. You see, equal opportunity for Black folks was at the core of the NAACP's mission.

Anyway, Mr. Pitts became very involved with our efforts to achieve equal employment at J&L Steel, and he was very familiar with the fact that J&L didn't seem to care much for equal opportunity when such involved the conception of including Blacks. He understood, as we did, that they would eagerly support equal opportunity when the minority was a woman of Caucasian origin. And so, the fight took a natural turn toward the courts.

In our fight to obtain equal employment opportunities for people of color, we filed approximately twelve claims with the EEOC. I must confess that I was surprised to see the Blacks that were in charge of the local Equal Employment Opportunity Commission branch assiduously sought ways to deny our claims.

Is it any wonder that we have been denied equal opportunity for so many centuries? It is a fact that Whites have been able to use our own Black folks to fight against equal opportunity for Blacks, even as far back as slavery. But *thanks be to God Almighty* that history has proven that some folks can't be bought with a fist full of dollars, smiles, and favors.

Dr. King had an advantage over many leaders because he approached his calling *without* the baggage of fear that most folks have. Well, you might ask, how does that work?

Think about it for a moment, and you will understand that down through history, some of our greatest leaders who fought the good fight were literally fearless leaders because they (1) fought with the conviction that what they were fighting for was righteous; (2) believed that their fight couldn't be avoided, and therefore they fought with insensitivity to their own plight; and finally, (3) the greatest fighters usually had a belief that the Creator, the God of Abraham, Isaiah, and Jacob, was with them. And should they lose their life, they would gain supernatural status with God, just as Paul declared to Timothy in 2 Timothy 4:7–8 (KJV):

> I have fought a good fight, I have finished my course, I have kept the faith: Henceforth there is laid up for me a crown of righteousness, which the Lord, the righteous judge, shall give me at that day: and not to me only, but unto all them also that love his appearing.

There were a few such fighters listed in the Scriptures. For instance, there was David who triumphed over Goliath. Daniel fought a spiritual war with Darius that resulted in a physical victory over the lion's Babylonians den. Joshua fought a battle at Jericho that was won with spiritual acts of shouting and crying out to God, which was infinitely more powerful than all of the enemies' swords and other contemporary weapons of war.

And so, we must note that the August 19, 1981, press conference was just one facet of the large battle that the J&L Black Caucus was waging to make necessary changes to a well-entrenched double-standard system that treated White people as privileged and Black people, basically, as second- and third-class citizens. It was a struggle just to get an ear to the president and those that served under his supervision.

One thing I found out very early in our quest for equal treatment: The president's subordinates worked tirelessly to give him the privilege of "plausible deniability." In other words, they sought to buffet him from any facts that they deemed could eventually cause him to get in trouble with certain government agencies. This was important because our company J&L/LTV was holding approximately fifteen billion dollars ($15,000,000,000) in federal government contracts. This was tax revenue dollars that came from all citizens. These contracts were tied to certain agreements that made false claims that our company was adhering to certain equal opportunity policies and specifically claimed that J&L/LTV did not discriminate on the basis of race, creed, color, etc. Our research indicated that the Office of Federal Contract Compliance Programs (OFCCP) was charged with oversight/enforcement capabilities. Through various consent decrees, this office was primarily designed to make the public believe that since the contractor (J&L/LTV) was making use of federal government funds that came from us, the taxpayers, said contractor would be held responsible for enacting equal opportunity in their (the contractor) respective workplace. And when violations were found, there would be certain redress or remedies, if you will; however, we found none. And when you think about it, you will understand how difficult it is for the privileged to even acknowledge to the underprivileged that their status quo mistreatment of them was and/or is wrong.

We were mentally charged and prepared to make every legal effort to be heard, so in the process, we learned a few things about the corporate mentally that would be useful in the way we were to deal with the higher echelons. (1) After almost all meetings with corporate officials on any level, when the subject was about racial equality, I would most assuredly write that individual a letter to confirm what was said. (2) These individuals never wanted the playing field to be equal, even when they would respond to you and consent to meet with you. They all emphasized the fact that they didn't recognize the group as an entity they would deal with. However, when a meeting was arranged with one of the vice presidents, they always insisted on having what I called "heavy backup." But I prayed to God about these meetings and came up with a strategy that was very effective in getting the attention of the top tier. I would almost always cc the president on almost all the hundreds of documents that I wrote. This tactic took away the president's privilege of plausible deniability. (3) I had to stand my ground and not allow them to engage in conversation with me about letters I had written to our group and those written to others that some "Uncle Tom" had passed on to them. (4) Some of my coworkers and colleagues were quite dismayed when I informed them that we had in our group at least one informant. However, being from rural Alabama, I was already prepared to deal with the reality that of some ninety or so individuals, there would be some who would sell their soul for thirty pieces of silver, and our group was certainly no exception. I had also learned from my previous experience in Alabama that it would probably not be worth the effort to spend time trying to figure out who the snitch was. You see, that was one of the most valuable essences of a good prayer life. No informant can hide from God. In case you haven't figured it out, the equality of employment we were seeking actually was the manifestation of the Holy Spirit working through us. As I have said elsewhere in this writing, when you are fighting against evil (spirits), you can't win without the Holy Spirit. Our Lord and Savior is not pleased when corporations or other entities, for that matter, who seek to discriminate against certain types of persons on the basics of so-called race.

God is no respecter of persons (meaning, God does not show favoritism).

> Then Peter opened his mouth, and said,
> of a truth I perceive that God is no respecter of
> persons: But in every nation he that feareth him,
> and worketh righteousness, is accepted with him.
> (Acts 10:34–35 KJV)

When we discriminate and treat others wrong, we offend God because God created us all, and consequently, He loves us all and wants us to obey His commandments. We are all aware that there are many scriptures telling us how to love and treat one another. One even tells us to love our neighbors as we love ourselves.

As I have indicated elsewhere, it is very difficult to eradicate systemic racial discrimination because it is so well favored by those in control. When you really think about it, you will understand that the controlling class wanted their children and future offspring to benefit as they did by not having to compete with whole races/classes of folks. For example, in 1969, when I came into the corporate structure at J&L Steel Corporation, there were a number of Whites who were situated in vice president's position without benefit of a college education. As affirmative action began to impact Corporate America, the standards were increased for at least two reasons: (1) Technology had advanced to a level that a college degree was becoming more essential in certain areas at the work place; (2) requiring a college education would slow the influx of Blacks coming into the corporate management world by virtue of limited financial resources available to them for college.

Let me be very clear about affirmative actions and just who we are talking about. Think about it: Even though the White establishment was able to push through legislation that declared White females were minorities, one would have to be crazy not to realize that the White ruling class would be more favorable to his White wife and White daughter than to a member of another class or race. Think about it for a minute, and you will soon realize, including

White females as minorities at that time simply watered down the affirmative action programs and, in many instances, brought in another class, if you will, that, given the opportunity, would add to the oppression/discrimination that was already prevalent in Corporate America. Everyone needs to take a hard and long look at the corporate work structure and know that whatever structure that is now in place was developed with the aid of (1) slavery and later 2.) a "Jim Crow" system that structurally denied Blacks basic human rights while grossly contributing to America's current financial status. It is, has been, and continues to be a fact.

Is there any wonder why Blacks have struggled so hard to be included in the dividends of a society that forced us to labor without pay, have their babies without consent, just to name a few of the familiar atrocities perpetrated by the White ruling class?

Our legal challenge

As indicated earlier in this writing, in 1981, we, the J&L Black Caucus, launched a barrage of complaints.

Before we march on with this discussion about our legal challenge, let me briefly explain what we were up against for the benefit of those who will read this account years after many changes have been made. and race discrimination will have ceased to be a relevant phenomenon. To show you what I am talking about, I will give you an excerpt from a January 30, 1981, *Wall Street Journal* written by Joann S Lublin. In this article, Lublin claimed that the then president Reagan's advisers wanted to drain much of the activism from the Equal Employment Opportunity Commission. She pointed out the fact that the agency under the Regan administration wanted us to believe that the EEOC has "created a new racism in America" by emphasizing affirmative-action quotas. *Is it any wonder why racial oppression has lasted so long!*

In this article, Ms. Lublin wrote about five suggestions that the transition team urged the new Regan administration to do: They would (1) impose a one-year freeze on lawsuits and new guideline introduced by the commission, (2) make it easier for employers to defend themselves (really, transition team? Do they need help to defend themselves against the most disenfranchised group in the United States of America?), (3) reduce the commission's budget, thus using a known tool to destabilize any agency, (4) remove restriction on the preemployment use of testing and biographical histories, (5) reconsider the commission's entire "affirmative action" approach. The aforementioned suggestions were put forth by Regan's EEOC transition team, led by Mr. Jay Parker, a Black conservative who said he was committed to fighting job discrimination, but he said, "We don't want discrimination causing more discrimination." *Is it any wonder why racial oppression has lasted so long!* Anyone reading the subject article could easily see that the Regan administration was certain to replace Eleanor Holmes Norton with someone who would give the appearance of wanting equal opportunity for all while staging a public persona would make the president's administration appear as though they were operating in an impartial manner and simultaneously ensuring that the EEOC become a government agency that facilitates status quo race discrimination policies. Such government sponsored efforts are the primary reason for this toxic race discriminatory environment lingering throughout the United States corporate industrial complex.

I want to emphasize the fact that we, the J&L Black Caucus, sort to bring substantive change to our company by appealing to the consciousness of the corporate hierarchy, starting at the very top officer, Mr. Graham. When one is attempting to make changes to a system of institutionalized oppressive practices, it will take much more than a few conversations and promises from lower-level management to see results. In order to effect real change, the orders must move from top downward. Having said that, below, I am going to start our review by introducing you to certain parts of our legal challenge. I will present to you with commentary on the second phase of our legal challenge because the first part involved filing race discrimination complaints with the department of EEOC, and they were generally very disheartening because by the time we started filing our complaints (approximately twelve of them), the agency had become simply a tool of the government that was now being used to fight against those who were alleging race discrimination. Our then president Ronald Regan (president from January 20, 1981, to January 20, 1989) saw to it that this agency would be so watered down with such term as reverse discrimination, which was designed to deflect attention away from real race discrimination.

In any case, somewhere in 1981, approximately nine Black Caucus members filed race discrimination complaints with the Pittsburgh office of EEOC.

All of those Black Caucus members who filed the EEOC charges, at first, were without benefit of legal counsel because we believed that this government agency was established to be an aid to those who felt they have suffered racial or other kinds of discrimination in the workplace or other parts of our great society. Consequently, we were under the impression that they would diligently seek to get to the facts and vigorously examine the claims/charges made, and thereby we would have means to address and possibly seek redress, where instances of corporate racial discrimination had been found.

The EEOC and the OFCCP proved to be very disappointing agencies to all of our complainants. Nevertheless, below I will offer a synopsis of the filers and subsequent results of their particular claims.

But let me offer a glimpse of the major obstacles we faced, even as we had put our faith in the integrity of these agencies and their perceived mission.

Early on, we realized that primarily the EEOC worked hard to prove that race discrimination was something that just didn't exist to a large extent. However, we heard about the Office of Federal Contract Compliance Programs (OFCCP), a regulatory agency that was supposed to ensure that companies holding major contracts with the federal government were in compliance with statutes dealing with all of the laws of the land and even laws and regulations that were supposed to prevent race discriminations.

Not knowing the internal rules and restrictive regulations between the EEOC and the Office of Federal Contract Compliance Programs (OFCCP), soon after filing complaints with EEOC, to our detriment, we filed similar complaints with OFCCP.

Below is a synopsis of the investigation process after the initial nine Black employees had filed race discrimination claims against J&L Steel Corporation. (Note that I'm using code designations to identify those individuals who participated in the process of seeking justice via filing claims.)

October 3, 1982, letter to Ms. Yvonne O'Conner of the US Department of Labor (with specific recommendations for substantive changes)

Dear Ms. O'Conner:

The J&L Black Caucus wishes to express its appreciation to you for giving us the opportunity to present our concerns. We hope the information we provide be useful in your appraising Senator Specter of the situation we are encountering at Jones and Laughlin Steel Corporation.

As we discussed, we feel the Caucus has been as forthright and specific as possible in presenting to the corporation what we considered to be realistic and viable solutions to unequal opportunity in J&L.

February 12, 1980, recommendations made to the vice president of industrial relations

The following list consists of requests and recommendations presented to Mr. J. H. Kirkwood, vice president of industrial relations, in a memorandum dated February 12, 1980. (See also a *summary of recommendations* presented to the general manager of personnel immediately after this letter.)

1. Please request that the chief executive officer of J&L inform everyone, via his annual videotaped progress report, that J&L is serious about affirmative action and therefore should channel all salaried job openings through the company's affirmative action officer or the individual serving in that capacity.

2. Require that the affirmative action officer approve new hires by actually reviewing and recording efforts made to achieve equal opportunity employment, not just by "rubber stamp," as have been the case in some previous situations.

3. Inform all J&L employees of the identity of the affirmative action officer.

4. Review the current nonexempt Black salaried workforce for possible promotions to the exempt ranks, as has been the case with some non-Blacks in J&L.

5. Require the same standards for all prospective employees. Suffice it to say, all non-Blacks do not fall into the excellent category—academically or otherwise.

6. Consider hiring a conscientious Black for the purpose of recruiting salaried exempt and nonexempt prospective employees. Implementing this suggestion would improve the hiring chances of Blacks because of the subjective element involved in the hiring process, allowing the interviewer and the interviewee to relate to one another on a very general basis.

7. Let J&L's affirmative action records be an open book, ready for review upon request by interested individuals within J&L and affiliated organizations.

8. Consider employing the services of minority-hiring agencies here in Pittsburgh.

Also attached are proposals orally presented to Mr. D. L. Carroll, general manager of personnel, on September 25, 1982. To date, and to the best of our ability to surmise, none of the recommendations has been implemented. The responses received from Mr. Kirkwood and Mr. Carroll indicated that they perceived the corporation's approach to establishing equal opportunity to be quite adequate. There is no evidence that the corporation recognizes the ineffectiveness of their practices.

It is our belief that if there is no intervention, any semblance of equal opportunity will never be achieved in J&L. To this end, we are most anxious to meet with Senator Specter.

Summary of recommendations submitted to D. L. Carroll, general manager of personnel, on September 25, 1982

A.   *Problem:* No Black representation in the top three levels of the corporation.

Proposal: Since the US Bureau of Census has determined that Blacks make up approximately 12 percent of the population, it is only fair that J&L work toward the goal of applying that percentage to the existing positions within the top three levels of the corporation. The results of this application would be used as targets or goals to strive for within a specified period of time as follows:

	Number of Positions		
	Present	Target (Blacks)	time period
First level from the CEO	14	2	2 yrs.
Second level from the CEO	69	8	2 yrs.
Third level from the CEO	217	26	3 yrs.

Progress reports would be presented at six-month intervals.

B.   *Problem:* Low retention rate for Blacks, particularly noticeable with Black management trainees.

From observation over the years, it appears that Black new hires fall into two categories:

1.   Competent and aggressive
2.   Incompetent

Individuals in the first category soon surmise that upward mobility is remote, and subsequently, they move on to corporations with more liberal traditions. Meanwhile, individuals in the second category are quickly terminated.

Proposal: The career path for Black employees should be closely tracked to determine if their path coincides with career objectives. If J&L is hiring quality individuals, then they should be willing to retain them, even when these individuals are Black. Part of the problem is due to the fact that not enough people in positions that are responsible for hiring, promotions, etc. feel that J&L is truly committed to the inclusion of Blacks in the so-called "Equal Opportunity Program" that we are told exists within J&L.

This attitude could be partially resolved with a few words from our president to the effect that he wants Blacks to share in the fruits of equal opportunity also.

C. *Problem:* Lack of high-level, nonexempt Blacks. Blacks, like other groups, want to experience advancement to the next level. However, the rate of advancement for Blacks in J&L is far below than that of their White counterparts.

Some areas seem to maintain what appears to be a standard percentage of Blacks.

Proposal: End immediately the use of different standards for evaluating and promoting Blacks and apply the same criteria across the board.

Eliminate the use of negative and discouraging stock phrases applied to Blacks exclusively, such as the following:

"You should have a college degree."

"You should have an advanced college degree."

"We just can't find a qualified Black for the position."

General solutions

A. Intensive executive recruiting, concentrating on large search firms.
B. Solicit the aid of Blacks already employed in J&L.

C. Pay the Black candidate on the same basis as White candidates.

D. Groom Blacks, as Whites are, through the corporate training program.

Summary

A few years ago, at the request of some disgruntled female employees, it was brought to the attention of the personnel department that a situation of sex harassment existed. It took less than a month for personnel to define the problem and institute what it deemed to be appropriate action. The point is that action was taken after the problem was identified.

One could wonder why this complaint was acted on so rapidly. I was given the reason, but I am aware that the complaints were made by mostly women of Caucasoid origin. You don't have to be a rocket scientist to know that upper management will act on a problem real fast when it involves members of their own race or group.

February 22, 1983, letter from US Department of Labor

On February 22, 1983, Ms. Annie A. Blackwell, area director of the US Department of Labor, OFCCP/ESA in Pittsburgh, Pennsylvania, sent a letter to me (HLM) reporting that she had visited the EEOC Office Pittsburgh area and was reporting the following findings:

She said, cases filed by (1) MHL and (2) WLE on February 26, 1982, were investigated by EEOC and were still open in the continuing investigation section.

(Note: [1] MHL: File EEOC claim in 1981 and later filed with OFCCP. The claim was found to be untimely. It didn't meet the requirements of the statutes of limitation for file time. This didn't mean that the case didn't have merit.)

(Again note: [2] WLE: File EEOC claim in 1981 and later filed with OFCCP. The claim was found to be untimely. Again, this didn't necessarily mean that the case didn't have merit.)

Ms. Blackwell further said that (3) JAO was closed by EEOC with a "no probable cause" finding.

(4) PEO was closed by EEOC with a "no probable cause finding."

(5) JAW was closed by EEOC with a "no probable cause finding."

(6) HBO was closed by EEOC with a "no probable cause finding."

(7) HGO was closed by EEOC with a "no probable cause finding."

(8) MGO's allegation was considered untimely by OFCCP because the alleged violations occurred at a time exceeding the 180-day statute of time limitation.

(9) WBO withdrew her complaint on January 17, 1983.

In the final paragraph of Ms. Blackwell's letter, she writes:

Through our investigation, it had been found that six of the complainants had filed identical charges with the Equal Employment Opportunity Commission, Pittsburgh area office, where an investigation and determination was rendered. One complainant's allegation was considered untimely and another withdrawn. Therefore, in keeping with a memorandum of understanding between OFCCP and EEOC, which prohibits a duplication of efforts, this department's processing of this complaint was hereby concluded.

Please note: The forgoing statement/argument that a memorandum of understanding between the two government agencies did effectively cause the OFCCP to preclude investigating our claims would have perhaps been justified *if* (1) only someone had informed us that such an administrative calamity existed between these two agencies and 2.) notwithstanding the fact that at least three of the subject cases that were determined to be without substance or (to use their terminology) "with a no probable cause" finding and yet were later adjudicated, and the complainants actually won their cases against J&L Steel Corporation. *Is it any wonder why racial oppression has lasted so long!*

March 19, 1983, letter to Senator Specter

Below is a March 19, 1983, *letter sent to US Senator Arlen Specter*, explaining in great details the pitfalls we encountered in dealing with the OFCCP.

Dear Senator Specter:

We are grateful to you and your staff for aiding us in our struggle to see that equal opportunity is realized at our company, Jones and Laughlin Steel Corporation (J&L).

However, we would be less than candid if we did not inform you of the gross injustices that have been perpetrated upon us by the Office of Federal Contract Compliance Programs (OFCCP).

Up front, we would like to concur, with certain reservations, with views President Reagan has expressed involving the dismantling of agencies, such as OFCCP. Since the president has decided that such agencies are not to have the administrative authority to perform real investigations of alleged race discrimination, why then are such offices staffed, at taxpayers' expense, with so many specialists who claim that they will investigate complaints of race discrimination.

In the writing that follows, we will give a synopsis of the injustices we have suffered while dealing with OFCCP.

On November 3, 1981, eight of our members filed a class complaint at the Pittsburgh area office of OFCCP (reference C810418), alleging race discrimination at Jones and Laughlin Steel Corporation involving promotion, downgrading, transfer, job assignment, harassment, and inadequate job profile. We further claimed that the overall situation was of a continuing nature.

Part of our prima facie case was based on a one-year study of the top three echelons of J&L. This comprehensive study covered a period from August 1, 1980, to August 1, 1981. Our study revealed that there were some 227 individuals in the Pittsburgh area in positions in the top three echelons, and within that year, there were forty promotions and ten new hires, yet none of the promotions or new hires was people of Black origin. Since there are no Blacks in this elite group nor have there ever been, one must conclude that our one-year study is indicative of the records for all the years prior to 1980 going back to J&L's formation. However, we were told in a February 24, 1983, meeting with OFCCP that they did not and will not investigate our complaint because of their own red tape and creative pitfalls. Consequently, J&L is allowed to carry on in its usual discriminatory manner while making much use of taxpayers' dollars.

After accepting our November 1981 complaints and using them to help justify their existence as an agency that supposedly serves the people by protecting their equal employment rights, we received a November 24, 1981, letter from the regional office that said that the Pittsburgh area office had been assigned our case and would being touch with us. The only response we received, until you intervened, was a May 20, 1983, letter, excusing their inaction by claiming staff limitations.

In 1981, Ms. Jane Harris, the OFCCP investigator assigned to our case, was very helpful in explaining OFCCP's procedures with respect to their acceptance of claims and subsequent investigations. We informed Ms. Harris of our intention to file the same charges with the Equal Employment Opportunity Commission (EEOC) and asked her if filing at EEOC would cause any problems with our cases already filed with OFCCP. Ms. Harris said that should we file the same race discrimination complaints with EEOC, there would be sharing of information by the two offices, but OFCCP would conduct its investigation independent of any EEOC investigation. She further made the distinction concerning the class action complaint we filed with OFCCP versus the individual complaints that would be filed at EEOC.

Ms. Annie Blackwell (director of OFCCP'S Pittsburgh area office) stated in our February 24, 1983, meeting that she assumed full responsibility for her investigator's failure to mention (on more than one occasion) that filing individual charges with EEOC, subsequent to the class complaint filed with OFCCP, would prelude an investigation. Ms. Blackwell stated, "That's most unfortunate." In other words, because of OFCCP'S mistake (creative pitfalls or what have you), they cannot investigate our case. Consequently, wanton (race) discrimination will continue to persist at J&L without a compliance or any other attempt to seek redress. Truly, we must wonder why such an agency does exist.

In the March 2, 1983, letter we received from Ms. Blackwell, reference is made to the notification of results of investigation. A review of the copy of these results (at this point, a reference was made to an exhibit B) is proof that OFCCP was only interested in determining ways to ensure that they would not investigate J&L. Please note the following:

1. OFCCP led us to believe that an investigation was already underway sometime in September of 1982; however, we subsequently learned that the investigation did not commence until January 1983. In a January 13, 1983, meeting with Messrs. Thomas and Larkin of OFCCP, we were informed that they had visited J&L for the first time the prior week. At that time, J&L attorneys pointed out to them that due to the fact that two of the complainants had filed a class action suit in federal court, OFCCP could not investigate our case. At this meeting, Mr. Thomas explained to us that had the complainants filed individual suit, OFCCP could have continued with its investigation.

    We had problems with these statements since the subject federal suits had not received class certification, and this did not represent class action suits. We informed OFCCP of this fact, and suddenly, any federal suit would preclude them from investigating. Bear in mind, we had informed OFCCP of our intentions to protect our right to sue by filing in federal court before EEOC's ninety-day expiration date. OFCCP *never* mentioned that such action would cause them not to perform an investigation.

2. In the March 2, 1983, letter, Mr. Blackwell (in paragraph 5, subparagraph 2) states, "A visit to the Pittsburgh area EEOC office revealed...cases filed with that agency by

Henry McNeil and Lorraine Williams on February 26, 1982, were investigated by EEOC and are still open in the continuing investigation section."

We are amazed that OFCCP would pretend that they had not already been informed of the foregoing fact. In fact, we sent to them copies of letters to EEOC in the fall of 1982, which showed the status of these cases.

3. In a December 21, 1982, phone conversation with Ms. Harris, we learned that OFCCP had reassigned our cases to Mr. Elijah Thomas. At first, this move seemed strange to us; however, the reason for this change is now quite clear. OFCCP changed investigators so that the gross inconsistencies and seemingly false statements would be revealed to us by new investigators (Messrs. Thomas and Larkin) and subsequently soften the blow, so to speak.

4. Paragraph 5 of the March 2 letter is erroneous. This paragraph states, "Six of the complainants have filed identical charges with the Pittsburgh area office EEOC, where an investigation and determination were rendered."

Fact: As of this writing, only five EEOC case determinations have been rendered while two are still in the continuing investigation section.

We feel taxpayers' dollars are being needlessly spent on an agency that was originally established to provide an avenue for addressing forms of discrimination, including race discrimination. We were told, given the go-ahead by the Department of Justice, that an investigation of our complaint would be performed. What we have dealt with is an agency that actively seeks ways not to investigate by hiding behind regulatory restraints that are virtually unknown to the public. For instance, how many of your constituents are aware of the following facts?

•   If a person files a complaint with one agency, it precludes an investigation by another agency, even if one complaint is individual and the other complaint is part of a class action complaint.

- If an individual files a federal suit (class or individual), such action would preclude an investigation by OFCCP.
- OFCCP will automatically accept EEOC, and the city of Pittsburgh Commission on Human Relations findings, even in the face of complainants' protest about the shabby or nonexistent investigative work conducted by these agencies.

In the February 24 meeting with OFCCP, Ms. Blackwell was eager to point out that she felt, because OFCCP did not issue a finding on any of the cases or the overall class action complaint, that OFCCP had thereby rendered a favor to us, the complainants, by not performing an investigation. She even stated, "You are better off by going into court without a finding from OFCCP."

Apparently, Ms. Blackwell, without any investigation conducted by her agency, has come to the conclusion that our complaints are frivolous and that the company, J&L, is in compliance with all applicable laws. While we suffer no such illusions, we would be satisfied with whatever findings and determinations that would result from a proper compliance review and an investigation of allegations made by us. We wonder why the OFCCP refused to investigate. Is it not their duty? If investigating race discrimination is not one of their duties, we would be pleased to find out what function they serve in our community.

We asked Ms. Blackwell if they would investigate our class action complaint if Henry McNeil and Lorraine Williams withdrew their complaints from EEOC. To this question, we have yet to receive an answer, even though Ms. Blackwell said she would discuss it the day after our meeting with her boss and get back to us with the results of that discussion.

It is tragic because of major misstatement of administrative policy that this agency purports to be one where US citizens can seek redress in class situation, such as ours, involving government contractors who are not exempt from Executive Order 11246, as amended.

Instead, LTV/J&L can continue to use more than six hundred million taxpayers' dollars a year in the face of extensive prima facie evidence of their racially discriminatory policies. We wonder what OFCCP'S real mission is. Taking into consideration what we have suffered at the hands of OFCCP, we feel that something is amiss. If this agency is not concerned about investigating race discrimination complaints, as is apparent, then the taxpayers' money should not be wasted on it. Instead, a modified agency should be established that would be allowed to investigate other forms of discrimination. This would simultaneously be a savings to the country and eliminate a facade.

Finally, Senator Specter, we feel that the injustices we have suffered from various acts and inactions by our company have been compounded by OFCCP'S refusal to investigate our complaint. If OFCCP had spent as much time investigation our claims as they did in seeking ways to avoid an investigation or a compliance review, we would not be compelled to write this letter. We are requesting a review of this situation, and we are still interested in a compliance review and/or a full-scale investigation of J&L's affirmative action practices with respect to Blacks. (End of letter to Senator Specter.)

As I indicated above, before our letter to the senator, at some point in 1981, approximately nine Black Caucus members filed race discrimination complaints with the Pittsburgh office of EEOC.

It is truly amazing how much effort Whites (over the years) have put into the mandate of maintaining the status quo. Yes, it's easy to see why those in power want to stay in power. However, I believe one can effectively hold on to power and be equitable with others in the distribution and cultivation of power simultaneously. Although, in order for such transition of status to exist, one has to be willing to submit to changes that will, in some cases, jeopardize the tremendous advantages such (White) individuals have held unfairly for so long.

What I find somewhat perplexing about race discrimination, both past and present, is that there are large segments of our society who label themselves as Christians and have made a confession of faith in the Lord Jesus Christ and say they love Jesus. However, these same individuals possess this extremely toxic and troubling spiritual persona that is exemplified and can be identified as nothing short of racial bigotry. And I might add that this persona is not limited to the Southern parts of the United States. When Mr. Trump came on the political scene, many Northern Whites decided it was time to step out and show their true identity. We all found out that even though the majority of the population now believe that determining a person's real abilities, potential, etc. should not be based on the color of that person's skin, it is still very difficult to give up that tremendous advantage when you are a part of the group that is receiving the benefits of such systematic long-standing unprovoked injustices and atrocities directed at primarily all non-White people. And some of the people in these sick-minded groups are folks of color themselves, now ain't that some troubling news? Suffice it to say, we Black folks have always known about Uncle Toms. But for some reason, today we are afraid to call them out.

Other stumbling blocks

Not only are we hampered from being able to get proper redress through EEOC and OFCCP, but consider what happened when in February 24, 1983, we, through the Freedom of Information Act, requested copies of J&L's equal employment opportunity, employer information reports (EEO-1). This was a report that would have shown the company's employee hiring statistics categorized by race and other such classifications. (Also note, a reference to this letter is in the prologue, page 11.)

We received a May 2, 1983, letter from the Employment Standards Administration, signed by the director, Ellen Shong Bergman, citing a 1979 US court decision that, in effect, shielded companies from revealing what they determined was confidential commercial information, saying that such revelations could cause commercial or financial harm.

A. Well, when companies are found to be at fault, and such revelations are discovered in the reports that they have submitted to the government, should they not be held responsible, even when that responsibility means that they should compensate the victims who have suffered because of their decision?

B. Not only should companies pay and be impacted financially because of their actions, specifically, they should be forced to compensate those victims affected by their unjust racial policies. The corporate sector of our society must need to feel such negative financial effect on their profits as this would serve as a deterrent for future misguided decisions of this kind but only if you consider systemic corporate racial discrimination inappropriate.

C. Why would the federal government say they will address corporate race discrimination in a serious manner while simultaneously allowing very large corporations to actually hide the results of what they say they are correcting? (Something is extremely rotten in Denmark.)

Is it any wonder why racial oppression has lasted so long in the corporate sector of our society?

A synopsis of the EEOC cases and their results

Of the nine race discrimination complaints filed, I will give you the final disposition of them all as explained below:

7HGO—Gwendolyn Howze filed a race discrimination claim against J&L Steel Corporation with the EEOC in April of 1981 and was closed by them, finding no probable cause in August 1982. However, in October 1981, she had filed a similar claim with OFCCP, which was not investigated by that agency because they used the excuse that two different agencies couldn't investigate "like" claims (a regulatory procedure that was not made known to us before we filed at both agencies). One of the most frustrating things about these various government agencies that were "fronting" as a help to the minority sector of our society was the fact that they seem to be always seeking ways to debunk any racial discrimination claims made by Blacks. I'm not sure what happens when the claimant is a

White female. The few claims we were victorious in were the results of intense attention by lawyers who were representing us and not by any of these government regulatory agencies.

Gwen wrote a July 21, 1983, letter to Mr. Webb, a member of the agency. In her letter, she makes at least five valid points worth mentioning: (1) in a predetermination interview conducted by the EEOC investigator with her (the complainant) while she was at work and setting in an open area surrounded by her coworkers was, to say the least, unobjective and inappropriate; (2) the agency deliberately avoided using new information offered by Gwen so that they could continue to support a "no cause" finding even when presented with new information; (3) the agency representatives were not ready to allow the charging party any room to suggest areas of concerns that they might review to better understand the issues being brought up; (4) Gwen presented much evidence that would easily show that she had superior experience when compared to the White counterpart in question, but it was summarily ignored; (5) Gwen concluded her final note saying that even after she had informed the investigators that the woman who had previously held the position in question was hired off the street and had no prior experience for the position, they held to their claim for not finding cause to rule in her favor. This led to her summation, where she expressed disappointment that an agency charged with protecting persons who find themselves in positions such as hers would render such a shoddy, biased investigation. She went on to say that unless there is immediate intervention to stop this practice, equal employment opportunity would die out in this century.

Cutting to the chase, Gwen's case was tried in September 10, 1984, in the US District Court of Western Pennsylvania, and this court ruled in favor of J&L Steel. However, on appeal, the Third Circuit US Court of Appeals in a December 28, 1984, ruling set aside the earlier ruling and allowed Gwen additional discovery time, and as a result, she won her case and was awarded a new job and ultimately received proper consideration and resulting compensation as well as relocation to another location within the company. *To God be the glory!*

It is worth noting that even though Gwen won her case, it was *not* won because of the government agencies working on her behalf, but rather, the court ruled in her favor *in spite of* the various government agencies fighting on behalf of the company. Gwen's case, and others like it, was the results of God's favor and group tenacity. *Is it any wonder why racial oppression lasted so long in the corporate sector of our society?*

3JOA—Alex Jones file EEOC claim in 1981 and later in February 26, 1982, was issued a right to Sue.

September 10, 1984, case was argued on appeal before US Court of Appeals for the Third Circuit, and an opinion filed on December 28, 1984, the Third Circuit Court of Appeals ruled that 3JOA was unjustly denied extended time for discovery (gathering of the evidence and facts for the case), which led to the subsequent granting summary judgment in favor of J&L. The appeals court noted that the company had the district court held that 3JOA had not established a prima facie case under Title VII because he had not shown to which jobs the younger White employees were promoted nor what qualifications the defendant company considered for any job promotion. But the appeals court pointed out the fact that it was J&L's policy not to post job openings or to specify the qualifications for a particular position. Hence, 3JOA's only recourse to obtain such information was through the discovery process. This higher court deemed it fair to allow charging party this opportunity, in light of the forgoing, and they also pointed out, J&L did not allege that it would be prejudiced if the court granted the motion to file an amended complaint, nor did it contest the motion to extend the period of discovery.

Again, it's worth noting that even though later, Alex (3JOA) won his case, it was not won because of the government agencies working on his behalf, but rather, the court ruled in his favor in spite of the various government agencies fighting (via their various delays and utter refusal to objectively investigate racial discrimination cases) on behalf of the company. Alex's case, and others like it, was the result of God's favor and group tenacity. *Is it any wonder why racial oppression lasted so long in the corporate sector of our society?*

5JAW-Anna Jones (wife of Alex) filed a job discrimination suit against J&L Steel Corporation with the EEOC and subsequently with the OFCCP in 1981.

Her case was closed by the EEOC on December 14, 1982. Then she took her case to the United States District Court for the Western District of Pennsylvania. Her lawyer was Attorney Thomas Henderson. She, being the plaintiff in this Title VII case, had the initial burden of establishing a prima facie case of racial discrimination, which she did by (1) belonging to a racial minority; (2) applying and being qualified for a job for which the employer was seeking applicants; (3) that despite her qualification, she was rejected; and (4) that after her rejection, the position remained open, and the employer continued to seek applicants from persons of complainant's qualifications. After establishing a prima facie case of racial discrimination, it became J&L's burden to adduce evidence that Anna was rejected, and someone else was preferred for a legitimate, nondiscriminatory reason.

The company said the decision to promote the other person (who was White) over Anna was based on his educational background and the evaluation process, which involved his supervisor's subjective impressions. The court held that J&L failed to meet its burden of production. The court went on to explain that since the selection and the evaluation process upon which J&L reached its decision are totally subjective in nature and because no accounting background or educational background levels had ever been or were requirements for the position she was seeking, it was clear that J&L failed even to meet its burden of production.

Note that in a December 16, 1982, letter I received from the EEOC area director about Anna and Gwen's cases that dealt with promotion, the EEOC said, "The EEOC nor charging party may substitute its judgment for that of the employer." However, as we will see below, that judgment must be brought under scrutiny because it was and often is bias. In fact, that was the presupposition or reason the agency was established in the first place.

Furthermore, the company proffered explanations, such as analytical ability and organization as support, for its decision are (in the court's words) thoroughly subjective, as was the evaluation process.

J&L also advanced education as a reason to rebut Mrs. Jones's prima facie case despite the testimony that neither a college degree nor accounting education was a requirement or qualification for the position. It was further noted that J&L's policies and practices did not permit Mrs. Jones to demonstrate her educational background, even though the person making the promotional decision was apparently ignorant of that background. Consequently, the court, after hearing all the evidence presented by J&L, concluded that based on the evidence presented, Anna demonstrated by a preponderance of the evidence produced at trial that but for her race, she would have been awarded the position in question. So after much prayer, supplication, and perseverance, Anna won her case in spite of the tremendous amount of opposition to racial equality in our workplace. *Is it any wonder why racial oppression lasted so long in the corporate sector of our society?*

The other six cases

As we said previously, nine cases were initially filed in 1981 with the EEOC, and subsequently, these same people filed with their race discrimination cases in 1982 with the Pittsburgh Office of Federal Contract Compliance Programs (OFCCP). Three of these cases were adjudicated as indicated above; however, below, we offer a brief analysis of the remaining six cases and their subsequent dispositions or the lack thereof.

The six cases were those filed by H. L. McNeil, Lorraine Williams, Elmer Patterson, Beatrice Hogan, George McCoy, and Billie Watkins.

1. 1MHL—H. L. McNeil's case was found to be untimely, a technicality that allows guilty parties to be void of responsibility if your lawsuit/accusation does not fall within the parameters of a certain time limit.

2. 2WLE—Lorraine William's case was also found to the untimely.
3. 4PEO—Elmer Patterson's case was not considered strong enough and thus was given a "no cause" finding.
4. 6HBO—Beatrice Hogan's case was not considered strong enough and thus was giving a "no cause" finding.
5. 8MGO—George McCoy's case was considered untimely.
6. 9WBO—Billie Watkins withdrew her complaint before it could be investigated.

Summary of a Few Accomplishments

Keep in mind that there were quite a few barriers that were taken down during this whole process, which we give all praise to God for. The list below is not an extensive list, but I have condensed this list for this particular writing effort.

Limited success via corporate administrative efforts

1. *February 1, 1979*—After reviewing a letter outlining Black Caucus complaints about unequal treatment at the worksite, an acting vice president of finance decided to investigate the accusations. After finding the complaints to be legitimate, he took the initiative to intervene in the hiring process at the Plaza, which resulted in more than twenty Blacks being hired in the clerical pool, and three Blacks were hired in the exempt (management) pool. See details in "(25) Postexile Fight" starting on pg 43.

2. *March 21, 1980*—The author was promoted to the position of area supervisor general and maintenance a Pittsburgh works accounting (equivalent to assistant controller) at the second largest works in our company.

Some success via federal court rulings

3. *November 9, 1981*—Caucus members began their legal struggle by filing (with EEOC) twelve claims of racial discrimination against J&L Steel Corporation.
4. *January 31, 1983*—OFCCP said they had issued two "right to sue" orders, which enabled the individuals to launch civil action in the federal court system.
5. *January 30, 1984*—We appealed the rulings of Alex's and Gwen's cases to the Third Circuit court of appeals.
6. *May 21, 1984*—Anna brought suit in the federal court against J&L for racial discrimination at the workplace.
7. *July 25, 1984*—Judgment entered in favor of Anna in the U.S. District court for Western Pennsylvania.
8. *September 10, 1984*—The US District Court for Western Pennsylvania granted summary judgment in favor of J&L Steel Corporation in the case of Alex and Gwen vs. J&L Steel.
9. *December 28, 1984*—The Third Circuit court of appeals set aside and overturned the district court's September 10, 1984, Alex and Gwen ruling.
10. *April 6, 1985*—The EEOC found cause to believe the Black Aliquippa guards were victims of race discrimination.
11. October 25 *1985*—Gwen accepted a new position at another location as part of the settlement of the civil right lawsuit she won.

It's worth noting that after these above cases were adjudicated in some manner, there was at least one race discrimination case filed in the late nineties, and the company (LTV) lost the case because of the facts presented before the federal judge.

The fight for equal rights at the workplace has been and will continue to be a difficult one, primarily because people like to have the advantage over those who are outside of their particular spear of influence.

Conclusion

Race Defined

I will conclude this writing by letting you know that the term *race* as we use in today's society is only 240 years old, and the designations of race that we use today were developed by *Johann Friedrich Blumenbach* (May 11, 1752–January 22, 1840), who was a German physician, naturalist, physiologist, and anthropologist. He was one of the first to explore the study of mankind as an aspect of natural history. His teachings in comparative anatomy were applied to the classification of what he called human races, of which he determined there to be five.

Blumenbach's work included his description of sixty human crania (skulls), published originally in fascicles as *Decas craniorum* (Göttingen 1790–1828). This was a founding work for other scientists in the field of craniometry. He divided the human species into five races in 1779, later founded on crania research (description of human skulls), and called them (1793/1795) the following:

- the Caucasian or White race
- the Mongolian or yellow race, including all East Asians and some Central Asians
- the Malayan or brown race, including Southeast Asian and Pacific Islanders

- the Ethiopian or Black race, including sub-Saharan Africans
- the American or red race, including American Indians[3]

One should understand that this classification was not designed by Mr. *Blumenbach* for the purpose of setting various people against each other, nor was his research/work designed to separate people into distinct classes so they could designate one class more intelligent than another.

Regardless of what Mr. Blumenbach's intentions were, the people in the Southern United States of America use these classifications to justify their raciest platforms and agendas. I must acknowledge that during the 1900s, there were large parts of the Northern US where race discrimination was practice, albeit ever so subtle.

---

[3] Wikipedia, Johann Friedrich Blumenbach.

About the Author

Giving all honor, praise, and thanks to our Lord and Savior, Jesus Christ, for allowing the author the opportunity to recall and expound on the subject matter in this way.

McNeil wants to posthumously thank his wife, Mrs. Leslie Carol McNeil, for being by his side during every step of the formation of this book.

Henry Leon McNeil was born in 1947 to the late Reverend Sol T. and Arnez E. McNeil in Mobile, Alabama; and while still a baby, the family moved back to his parents' hometown of Camden, Alabama.

He was brought up in a Christian home in the rural environment of the Hills (as that part of the community was referred to at that time) of Camden, Alabama.

His inspiration for writing this book started when, after pursuing a career in the business world in 1969 at J&L Steel, he soon discovered that a major part of what he was witnessing was subtle and overt racial discrimination being practiced in the company where he was employed as a young potential corporate executive.

Prior to migrating to the northern part of our country, he was misinformed by his kinfolk and acquaintances who had been raised in the north. They had given him the distinct impression that race discrimination was so rare in the North that they hardly gave notice of such. But when he arrived, he found a very different reality, and that is why he was prompted to launch a movement to challenge some of the more obvious institutionalized acts of corporate race discrimination.

McNeil gives thanks to God that we live in a democratic society/ government, where we can criticize those who serve in high corporate and government positions and not be killed for having done so.

To God be the glory. Precious is His name.

Rev. H. L. McNeil, daughter, Nicene R. McNeil and wife, Leslie C. McNeil.

My daughters Lauren and Nicene at the restaurant together.